DEFENSES OF NARRAGANSETT BAY IN WORLD WAR II

OTHER BOOKS BY THE AUTHOR:

The Hessian Occupation of Newport and Rhode Island, 1776-1779

Stars and Swastikas; The Boy Who Wore Two Uniforms

Dutch Island and Fort Greble

Davisville and the Seabees

DEFENSES OF NARRAGANSETT BAY IN WORLD WAR II

BY
WALTER K. SCHRODER

RHODE ISLAND PUBLICATIONS SOCIETY

RHODE ISLAND PUBLICATIONS SOCIETY

Dr. Patrick T. Conley, *Chairman*
Professor Robert J. McKenna, *Secretary*
Mary Brennan
Paul R. Campbell
Dr. Joel A. Cohen
Albert T. Klyberg
Mildred Longo
Professor D. Scott Molloy
Dr. Paul F. O'Malley
House Speaker Matthew J. Smith
Captain Ronald G. Tracey

Hilliard Beller, *Editor*
Gail C. Cahalan, *Office Manager*
M. Helena Lopes, *Bookkeeper*
Phyllis Cardullo, *Secretary*

Copyright © Rhode Island Bicentennial Foundation 1980
All Rights Reserved, Printed in the U.S.A.

Library of Congress Catalog Card Number: 80-51763
ISBN: 0-917012-22-4

Edited by Steven Strang and Hilliard Beller

First Printing—September 1980
Second Printing—December 1980
Third Printing—July 1983
Fourth Printing—December 1987
Fifth Printing—April 1993

Sixth Printing—December 1994
Seventh Printing—October 1996
Eighth Printing—January 1999
Ninth Printing—April 2002
Tenth Printing—May 2006

No part of this publication may be reproduced, stored in a retrieval system, or transmitted, in any form or by any means, electronic or mechanical, including photocopying and recording, without permission in writing from the publisher, except by a reviewer who wishes to quote brief passages for a review to be included in a magazine, newspaper, or broadcast.

Printed by PROFESSIONAL PRESS, Chapel Hill, North Carolina

Photo Credits:
Front Cover: 8-inch Battery Reilley, Fort Church.
  Photo CDR C. Robbins, courtesy U.S. Army Casemate Museum
Back Cover: Antisubmarine defenses in East Passage.
  National Archives photo 80-G-452349

Dedicated to the thousands of men and women who served the Armed Forces in the Narragansett Bay Area during the Second World War.

Foreword

The formal publication of this excellent history of the Defenses of Narragansett Bay in World War II is of inestimable value to the education of Rhode Islanders who were not privy to the very large part our State played in that conflict. Further, this volume encompasses an outstanding delineation of the Federal service of the 243d Coast Artillery Regiment, Rhode Island National Guard, during the period, for which I personally am very grateful.

In my original reading of Walter K. Schroder's history of the Defenses of Narragansett Bay in World War II and the stories of the soldiers, sailors and airmen who manned them, I was reminded of the full scope of John Milton's famous and oft quoted phrase "Thousands at his bidding speed, and post o'er land and ocean without rest; they also serve who only stand and wait." For so they did, these defenders of Narragansett Bay in World War II; they prepared, stood fast and waited and waited and waited.

It is most important that we not forget that these fortifications and those who manned them were in Rhode Island in great numbers and that both men and materiel were well prepared to thwart any attempted invasion of our shores.

The conduct of great invasion battles makes thrilling reading, but the essence of success in coastal defense is thorough planning and the patience and strength to overcome the tedium of seemingly endless and meaningless practice. The truly successful Coastal Defense Force is the one which masters that particular aspect of the military art to such a degree that its strength is so widely respected, ... it is never tried.

So it was with the coastal defenses of Narragansett Bay — the physical preparation, the devotion to duty, the diligent practice, the long nights and days of patient alert waiting, all paid the highest dividend — the defenses were not tried and the specter of war was not visited upon our shores.

To those brave, devoted and diligent men and women who served in the United States military in defense of our beautiful bay through the long years of the Second World War, wherever you may now be, I salute you. To all others, I highly recommend Walter K. Schroder's detailed account of their service and sacrifice.

LEONARD HOLLAND
Major General
Adjutant General of Rhode Island

Preface

My decision several years ago to research the World War II period in the Lower Narragansett Bay area was prompted by simple curiosity coupled with an urge to learn more about that area's silent concrete and steel remains, evidence of a military buildup and presence of considerable magnitude in our coastal area. The appearance of some of these sites today gives few clues as to their true age, and invariably the casual observer will associate these now-abandoned defense installations with the World War II, or perhaps World War I, period. That impression may be correct in some instances; however, a number of Narrragansett Bay forts still existing in what are now for the most part public recreational areas were built around the turn of the century — with Fort Adams antedating these by many decades. Not until I seriously delved into the available information did I realize that even the older fortifications were actively used by the military during World War II. With the addition of more modern facilities during the war years, the entire southern shoreline of Rhode Island was eventually protected by a completely coordinated system of heavily fortified areas, troop encampments and support facilities, all designed and integrated to guard the Bay against enemy incursion. Behind this protective umbrella, the first line of our continental defenses, the Navy was feverishly at work enlarging existing facilities or building new ones while training hundreds of thousands of men at several installations within the Bay for service with the expanding fleet.

World War II is now history. The ranks of the many Rhode Islanders who served with the military contingents assigned to these defenses are slowly thinning out. Their sons and daughters, the occasional visitor — in fact, a whole new generation now views the mute and crumbling monuments of that era and wonders: What was their significance?

As I pause in the ruins of a deserted command bunker and envision the barbed wire, machine gun emplacements, and, above all, the long black gun barrels pointing to the sea, I realize that all this was deadly serious just a few short years ago. That point was made adequately clear when I learned that the enemy brought disaster within sight of Army ground observers at Point Judith, necessitating decisive naval action in Rhode Island waters just hours before cessation of hostilities on the European continent.

Ultimately, several of the Narragansett Bay forts became the center of the most ambitious long-range prisoner of war re-education efforts ever to be undertaken by the United States, a project shrouded in secrecy for many months. Thus, the Narragansett Bay area had its own unique wartime experiences, a story worth telling and recording.

The compilation of data which follows is based primarily on official records retrieved from various governmental archives and agencies, supplemented by information acquired from eyewitnesses and other creditable sources. My purpose has been to assemble in one place the available information illustrated by many heretofore unpublished photographs and other materials for the benefit of those who also might be interested in knowing more of that period in the 1940's when the Rhode Island National Guard and other Army units manned the harbor defenses of Narragansett Bay. Their presence provided the fighting forces with the security and the time required to prepare to meet the enemy on battlefields far from our own shores.

Information from many individuals and agencies was used to formalize this record. Among these sources a number of persons were especially helpful. First and foremost I wish to acknowledge the assistance of the late Lt. Col. John C. Rembijas, USA (Ret.), who recounted his experiences as an officer of the 243rd Coast Artillery Regiment for me during several discussions and visits to the formerly fortified areas. Special thanks are due Alfred K. Schroeder, photographer and member of the Council on Abandoned Military Posts (CAMP) for making available his extensive collection of photographs. His interest and help were truly invaluable. I wish to express my appreciation also to George E. Howarth, R. I. Department of Environmental Management and Chairman, New England Department of CAMP, for sharing his intimate knowledge of the history of Fort Adams with me; to Judith M. Gansberg, author, for providing a listing of suggested informational sources; to Colonel Maxwell S. McKnight, USA (Ret.), and Professor William Moulton, Ph.D., Princeton University, for their comments regarding the PW Schools; to Donald C. Rhodes, son of Lt. Col. Frank B. Rhodes, Jr., 243rd Coast Artillery Regiment, who on many occasions willingly recalled names and events involving the Regiment and Fort

Wetherill; to Lauretta Smith, wife of the late Lt. Col. Alpheus Smith, USA (Ret.), former Commandant of the PW School at Fort Getty, for allowing me to review her husband's scrapbook; to Professors Karl J. R. Arndt, Ph.D., Clark University, and Aubrey Parkman, Ph.D., Tufts University, for their contributions of information; to Charles H. Bogart for providing a discussion of Harbor Defense Command Structure; to Mrs. Catharine M. Wright for her suggestions and kind words of encouragement; and to Charles E. Brothers and Walter Vachon, both former members of the 243rd Coast Artillery Regiment, for offering their recollections on several occasions.

I also wish to thank W. M. Getchell and F. W. Pernell of the Reference Branch, General Archives Division, National Archives and Records Service, Washington, D.C., for their exceptional cooperation and support in retrieving records for me during the research phase of the project; Susan Berman, Reference Librarian, North Kingstown Free Library, for coming up with those hard-to-find books and references whenever availability was critical; and Ruth Lampel, Librarian, Jamestown Philomenian Library, for ready access to local resource materials on a continuing basis.

To the professionals who gave of their valuable time to assess the manuscript or portions thereof at various stages of completion and offered suggestions in their fields of expertise, I extend my sincere gratitude. Their criticisms as well as their remarks on the merits of the project were most helpful and appreciated. I wish to recognize these personalities in alphabetical order: Professor John B. Hattendorf, Historian, Naval War College; Brigadier General John W. Kiely, USA, Assistant Adjutant General for the State of Rhode Island; Dr. Emanuel R. Lewis , author and Librarian, House of Representatives; Anthony S. Nicolosi, Curator, Naval War College Museum and Historical Collection; Professor Harold Payson, Captain, USN (Ret.), Department of Science, Roger Williams College; and Professor James E. Schevill, Ph.D, Department of English, Brown University.

Very special thanks go to Mrs. Dorothy Cummings for deciphering and typing the several versions of the basic and revised manuscripts from exceptionally poorly handwritten originals without giving up; and to Mr. Steven Strang of the English Department at Brown University for accepting the challenge of editing the manuscript and maintaining a patient and positive attitude throughout the process.

My hat is off to my dear wife Lora and daughter Leah for being so cooperative and supportive of my endeavors over a long period of time. They are both to be complimented for being such patient and good listeners even when the subject discussed was a repeat of an even earlier re-hash.

WALTER K. SCHRODER

Jamestown, Rhode Island
May 15, 1980

TABLE OF CONTENTS

	FOREWORD	vii
	PREFACE	ix
I.	THE SETTING	1
	War in Europe	
	American Reactions	
	U.S. Continental Defenses	
	Geography of Narragansett Bay	
	Existing Narragansett Bay Defenses	
II.	PERIOD OF UNCERTAINTY	6
	Call to Duty	
	The Prewar Batteries	
	Fort Adams	
	Fort Wetherill	
	Fort Getty	
	Fort Greble	
	Fort Kearney	
	Prospect Hill Fire Control Station	
	Supply Lines	
III.	A NEW GENERATION OF SEACOAST FORTIFICATIONS	37
	The World War II Batteries	
	Fort Church	
	Fort Greene	
	Fort Burnside	
	Harbor Entrance Control Post	
	Fort Varnum	
	Minor Installations	
IV.	ARMY COAST AND HARBOR DEFENSE UNITS	67
	Evolution of Command	
	Shifting Priorities	
V.	WITHIN THE BAY	72
	Naval Expansion	
	Naval Training Station	
	Naval Torpedo Station	
	Naval Operating Base	
	Naval Fuel Depot	
	Naval Net Depot	
	Motor Torpedo Boat Squadrons Training Center	
	Naval Air Station	
	The Davisville Complex	
	Antiaircraft Defenses	
VI.	ENEMY NEARBY	97
	The Dark Days	
	A Time of Reckoning	
	Unrealized Potential	
	Selected POWs with a Mission	
	APPENDIX	120
	BIBLIOGRAPHY	123
	INDEX	129

PART I

The Setting

WAR IN EUROPE
A state of war began in Europe when German forces attacked and crossed into Poland in the early morning hours of September 1, 1939. Two days later Great Britain, France, Australia, New Zealand and India declared war on Germany, followed by South Africa on September 6 and Canada on September 10.

The war in Europe expanded rapidly. Italy joined forces with the Germans in June 1940. By the end of the summer, the German army had defeated Poland, subjugated Denmark and Norway, overrun Holland, Luxembourg and Belgium, forced France into capitulation, and had dealt a heavy blow to British expeditionary forces at Dunkirk.

AMERICAN REACTIONS
One of the initial reactions by the United States to the European War was the issuance of a presidential order to the Navy on September 5, 1939, to organize a Neutrality Patrol. The stated purpose of the patrol was to report and track all aircraft, ships and submarines belonging to the belligerents that approached both the U.S. coast and the West Indies. This naval activity was also intended to emphasize the readiness of the United States to defend the Western Hemisphere. A second proclamation banned the shipment of arms to the belligerents. On September 8, the President declared a limited national emergency. In the Act of Panama, issued on October 2, 1939, the nations of the Americas announced the united policy of keeping the European War from the New World and warned against conduct of any warlike operations by the belligerents in specifically identified areas off the North and South American continents. The Act in effect created a 300-mile Neutrality Zone which would be patroled by the U.S. Navy.

The President of the United States had been apprehensive of the possible threat to American security which would result from a German seizure of the Atlantic Coast of France. Since the British Navy had been relied upon for many years to prevent any dominant European power from controlling the Atlantic shipping lanes, the United States had concentrated its own naval forces in the Pacific. The dramatic changes in the European military situation during 1940 greatly increased the possibility of a German invasion of Great Britain which, if successful, would gravely threaten the sea lanes of the Atlantic and the security of the United States. Growing awareness of this danger led to implementation of a major naval expansion program in June of that year and the appropriation of several billion dollars in July to establish a "Two Ocean Navy" with resultant strengthening of U.S. naval forces committed to the Atlantic area.

U.S. CONTINENTAL DEFENSES

The Army's harbor and coastal defenses at that time consisted primarily of a series of pre-World War I fortifications concentrated near and for the defense of naval shore establishments and fleet anchorages. These facilities represented the existing landbased defenses of the continental United States and would require substantial reinforcement through mobile seacoast artillery as well as strong air and fleet support in the event of war. United States harbor defenses had long been recognized as being inadequate. They had been constructed around the turn of the century when little thought was given to protection from aerial bombardment. Moreover, most of the seacoast guns still in operation at these sites lacked the range of the more modern shipborne armaments.

In the 1930's various coast and harbor defense modernization plans had been proposed, but the limited funds available to implement these projects were used for the most part to bolster the continental defenses along the Pacific coast. Larger appropriations were forthcoming, however, as the threat of war in Europe became more imminent, and work to improve coastal defenses on the Atlantic was resumed with greater urgency. In May 1940, the Chief of the Coast Artillery noted: "With but few exceptions our seacoast batteries are outmoded and today are woefully inadequate. Nearly every battery is outranged by guns aboard ship that are of the same caliber. More alarming than this is the fact that every battery on the Atlantic Coast, and all but two of the batteries on the Pacific Coast, have no overhead cover so are open to attack from the air." At the time of France's downfall in mid-1940, the land-based defenses of the continental United States were undergoing further review and study.

GEOGRAPHY OF NARRAGANSETT BAY

The southerly approach to Rhode Island Sound, Buzzards Bay, and Vineyard Sound from the Atlantic Ocean is a 30-mile wide, deep and open waterway which is free of natural obstructions until one is close to land. The entrance to Narragansett Bay lies between Brenton Point on the east and Point Judith on the west. The length of the Bay from this entrance to the northern extremity of the mouth of the Providence River is approximately 20 miles. It is the approach by water to the cities of Newport, Providence, Fall River, and Taunton, as well as to the naval facilities in the lower Bay area. The average width of Narragansett Bay is five miles and good anchorage may be found almost anywhere. Conanicut and Prudence Islands lie within the Bay and divide it into two channels known as the East and West Passages. The East Passage is the deeper of the two and is also the more direct route to Newport.

Block Island Sound is a deep navigable waterway which forms the eastern approach to Long Island Sound from the Atlantic. It has two entrances from the ocean, an eastern entrance between Block Island and Point Judith and a southern entrance between Block Island and Montauk Point, Long Island. The breakwaters at Point Judith form a Harbor of Refuge for coastal traffic.

EXISTING NARRAGANSETT BAY DEFENSES

Five permanent forts guarded the entrances to Narragansett Bay. Fort Adams, constructed in the mid 1800's and situated on Newport Harbor, was the oldest fort in use and the easternmost. Upgraded through the addition of several external batteries after 1871, it commanded the East Passage in concert with the gun batteries of Fort Wetherill on Conanicut Island, constructed at the turn of the century. The West Passage was also controlled by older batteries located at Fort Getty on Conanicut Island, at Fort Greble on Dutch Island in the middle of the channel, and at Fort Kearney, the westernmost, located on the mainland. All of these sites had been utilized during World War I. By 1938 much of the original armament of these batteries had been removed as nonessential to military needs and all but Fort Adams were being held in an inactive caretaking status. The 10th Coast Artillery Regiment, a Regular Army unit based at Fort Adams since 1924, guarded and maintained the existing facilities.

East Passage in 1941. Newly constructed barracks at Fort Wetherill can be seen at left.

Photo courtesy of A. K. Schroeder, CAMP.

Additional lands at Point Judith and Sakonnet Point in Little Compton had been acquired by the Government in 1939 and earmarked as future sites of modern seacoast batteries.

It was into this environment that the 243rd Coast Artillery Regiment of the Rhode Island National Guard was inducted in September 1940. For the next five years the Narragansett Bay area was to be a beehive of military activity.

PART II

Period of Uncertainty

CALL TO DUTY

On August 27, 1940, the President called the Army Reserve and the National Guard into Federal Service. In response to this order, members of the 243rd Coast Artillery Regiment, a harbor defense unit, mustered at their assigned National Guard armories throughout the State of Rhode Island on September 16, 1940. The avowed purpose of the call-up was to engage in a one-year period of intensive training. The first few days after the call-up were devoted to processing personnel, completing physical examinations, checking out weapons and equipment, and preparing for movement to Fort Adams in Newport, from whence the Regiment would eventually be dispersed and assigned to permanent duty stations at existing fortified areas in the lower Narragansett Bay area.

On Sunday, September 22, prior to departing for their initial assignment, the 955 men and 66 officers of the Regiment, comprising units from Bristol, East Greenwich, Natick, Pawtucket, Providence, Westerly and Woonsocket, paraded through the capital city for a final review before senior officers and high-ranking state officials including Governor William H. Vanderbilt. Weighted down with full field packs and rifles, the troops formed at the Cranston Street Armory early in the day and marched toward the Providence County Courthouse, where the official review took place. The column was headed by Colonel Earl C. Webster, Commanding Officer, Lt. Colonel John F. Datson, Executive Officer, and members of their immediate staff. The regimental colors and the massed flags which followed were flying the many battle streamers which were emblematic of the Regiment's numerous earlier engagements. An estimated 100,000 flag-waving and cheering men, women, and children lined the parade route through downtown Providence. The excitement and the turnout were reminiscent of the large troop movements of World War I.

A crowd of 30,000 had gathered near the County Courthouse to witness the review of the massed battalions and to see the men off. It was the day on which the subordinate elements of the 243rd came together to enter the federal service as a single unit, the first such large complement to be inducted from the ranks of the Rhode Island National Guard.

Soon after the review and last minute farewells from family members, the troops mounted pre-assigned trucks from among 80 military vehicles drawn up at the end of the parade route and proceeded in convoy formation to Newport, their first official duty station. Upon debarking at Fort Adams that afternoon, the men were quickly assigned to temporary billets in tents that had been set up at the Citizens' Military Training Camp outside the fort. Hundreds of Newporters turned out to welcome the Regiment. In the days that followed, the Regiment lost no time in getting down to business. Infantry and artillery drills, physical conditioning, hikes, and specialized instruction became the order of the day.

The mere induction of the Guard and eventual activation of existing gun batteries in the Bay area did not of themselves assure the existence of an effective and integrated harbor defense force and system, however. The manning of base end stations at the flanks of the various gun batteries and the training of the observers assigned to these positions, for instance, were crucial because the transmission of accurate information by these men to the battery plotting rooms was a prerequisite to generating accurate aiming data for the gun crews. Raw data fed into the plotting rooms by several spotters observing the same target from different sites and angles made possible the pinpointing of a target through triangulation. In addition, by repeating this process at predetermined intervals, it was possible to predict a target's location, speed and direction or course at the end of the next time cycle. During this time lapse, factors such as rotation of the earth, curved trajectory and the time in flight of the projectile, the effects of tides, wind, waves, and the temperature of the gun powder were all taken into account. Then the converted or corrected data was relayed to the gun crews electronically for immediate application in preparing to fire. Just as important as the spotting of the target was the recording of the impact area of each round fired. Such information allowed further corrections to be made before the next round was expended.

There were many other factors to be considered and more

training to be accomplished before the harbor defense system was truly operational and ready for all eventualities. Training in mining the harbor, situating searchlights at critical points around the Bay, preparing for defense against smaller and speedy seagoing craft with hit-and-run capabilities as well as against the stealthy submarine, camouflaging the positions against aerial and ground observation, and installing antiaircraft defenses — all were high on the list of priorities. Several months after the unit was activated, 155mm field artillery pieces were assigned to the 243rd and emplaced at several strategic points along the shore.

The Panama Detachment, a regular army unit of 500 men which had been in training at Fort Adams for a year, was at that time preparing to ship out for duty in the Canal Zone. Within days of their arrival, the 243rd relieved the regulars and assumed the guard function at this post. The 10th Coast Artillery Regiment assigned to Fort Adams for many years was considerably under strength at that time. Battery 'A' was engaged in mine-planting operations in a designated area of the East Passage as part of its own training mission.

During an inspection on September 30, 1940, Major General James A. Woodruff, Commander of the First Corps Area, announced that the ranks of the 243rd would be bolstered through the addition of some 300 recruits. Construction of new military cantonments at Forts Wetherill and Getty progressed with great speed to ensure the units could be moved into permanent quarters before the winter. So extensive was the effort of preparing the new encampments across the Bay on Conanicut Island that area newspapers at that time spoke of the "mushrooming of two more cities in Rhode Island." Not only were barracks being erected, but all the other facilities incidental to sustaining large troop complements also were being built, including mess halls, medical and administrative spaces, day-rooms, a fire station, a theater, a post exchange, officers' quarters, and covered supply and storage areas.

Units of the 243rd moved into their new homes during the period October-December 1940, while hundreds of civilian construction workers were still laboring feverishly to complete the remaining work.

Lt. Colonel Ernest W. Moore, Commander of the 1st Battalion, moved to Fort Getty. Individual units assigned to that area included the regimental headquarters, Batteries 'A' and 'B' of Providence, the Searchlight Battery from East Greenwich, the Medical Detachment and the regimental band.

Meanwhile, Batteries 'C' of Bristol, 'D' of Providence, 'E' of Westerly, and 'F' of Woonsocket were asigned to Fort Wetherill under Lt. Colonel Frank B. Rhodes, Jr., Commander, 2nd Battalion. The 3rd Battalion, commanded by Lt. Colonel John L. Daneker, remained at Fort Adams, where Batteries 'G' of Providence, 'H' of Pawtucket, and 'I' of Natick were moved to enclosed areas vacated at the old Fort by the Panama Detachment.

During the early months of 1941 the number of troops assigned to the 243rd increased to a total of 1,665 men as a result of the addition of 600 Selective Service draftees, mostly Rhode Islanders. During this time the 10th Coast Artillery Regiment was also approaching its full strength of 1,150 men by supplementing the regulars with newly inducted personnel.

THE PREWAR BATTERIES

With few exceptions, the origin of the fortifications activated in the Narragansett Bay area in September 1940 can be traced to what is known as the Endicott construction period. This building phase had been preceded by investigations of a joint civilian and military board under the chairmanship of Secretary of War William C. Endicott, designated by Congress in 1885 to study and report on the status of the coastal and harbor defenses of the United States. Following submission of the board's findings and recommendations in January 1886, Congress in 1888 authorized the production of required seacoast artillery pieces and, in 1890, the construction of permanent gun and mortar batteries. Large-scale construction, however, did not get under way until 1896/97, with the majority of "Endicott Period" batteries in New England completed about 1906. It was during this time that the majority of the permanent batteries in existence in the Narragansett Bay area in 1940 came into being, with the exception of Fort Adams proper. Endicott batteries generally were designed for two or three weapons, each gun with a separate platform protected on three sides by concrete walls 15 to 20 feet thick. These massive structures were further protected on the exterior by parapets of sand with a thickness of 40 feet or more, covered with earth, and seeded or planted to blend with the terrain. Ammunition vaults were located at a lower level under the parapet adjacent to the gun platforms, with powder and shells moving to the platforms via mechanical hoists. The concrete structures also housed plotting rooms, offices and communications equipment. The guns in some instances

Typical Endicott Period fortification. Here, 12-inch Battery Varnum at Fort Wetherill.

National Archives photo 38-FCD-32.

Lower level of Endicott Period fortification. Gun emplacements were above.

National Archives photo 77-CD-23J.

were of the disappearing type which were exposed above the parapet only while firing. When built, the Endicott batteries were of the latest design and unsurpassed by any other coastal defense system then in existence. However, the great advances in naval weaponry and tactics during World War I soon made these static defenses vulnerable to attack from the sea. The development of aircraft as an instrument of war compounded the problem even further, since Endicott batteries provided neither overhead protection against aerial attack nor camouflage against aerial observation.

Fort Adams

Constructed during the period 1824-1857, Fort Adams was located about three miles southwest of the center of Newport on a peninsula projecting northward from Newport Neck, surrounded on three sides by the waters of Brenton Cove, Newport Harbor and the East Passage of Narragansett Bay. The 21½-acre granite, brick and earthen complex was part of a larger 136-acre reservation. The construction site was purchased by the Government in 1799-1800, with additional lands added in 1824. The Fort derived its designation from earlier defensive works at the same site that had been named Fort Adams on July 4, 1799, in honor of John Adams, the second President of the United States, who was then in office.

One of the largest and most elaborate seacoast fortifications of its time, Fort Adams was designed to mount 468 cannon with a wartime complement of 2,400 troops. It had been sited and engineered with a capability of engaging and destroying ships under sail seeking forced entry into the Bay, withstanding naval bombardment by small-bore cannon, and prevailing in a siege by ground forces. Yet, with the development of more powerful cannon and steam-driven ships of shallow draft during the Civil War, the Fort soon became obsolete as a viable harbor defense installation. Due to the strategic position of this land, however, several modern exterior batteries were constructed along the shore to the south of the Fort in the late 1800's, while 12" mortar batteries were installed further inland on the reservation.

Fort Adams had been an active military post since its very inception, having served as a staging area for troops during World War I and as home of the 13th Infantry Regiment from 1928-1939. The 10th Coast Artillery Regiment had occupied this post since 1924. By the time the 243rd Coast Artillery Regiment arrived in September 1940, the arma-

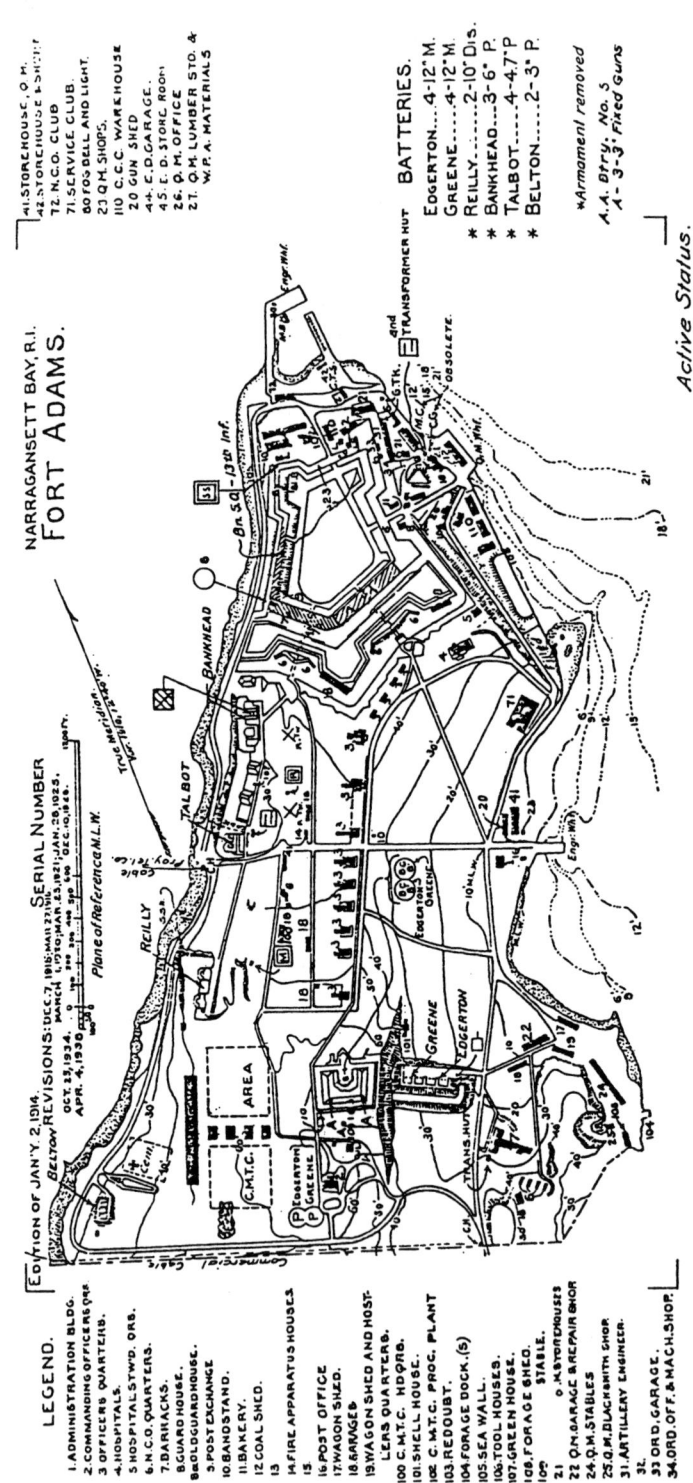

Source: National Archives Record Group 407 (Declassified NND 760162)

ments of the Fort and its exterior batteries had long been removed because of obsolescence. Only the 12" mortars and three 3" guns of a fixed antiaircraft battery remained. The mortars were salvaged in 1942.

Fort Adams, 1906. Firing of 12-inch mortars in the presence of Naval observers.

Photo courtesy A. K. Schroeder, CAMP.

Fort Adams in 1921.

National Archives photo 38-FCD-1.

Fort Adams in 1974. Exterior battery positions at right. Abandoned 12-inch mortar emplacements near center top.

Photo by A. K. Schroeder, CAMP.

Fort Wetherill

Fort Wetherill was located off Ocean Street on the southeastern shore of Conanicut Island, roughly two miles across the East Passage from Newport. The site was formerly known as "The Dumplings" and "Fort Dumplings" after a group of small islands nearby.

The original reservation was purchased by the Government in 1799, with additional lands added via condemnation during the period 1898-1902. The reservation comprised 61.5 acres. In 1900, the area was named in honor of Captain Alexander M. Wetherill, U.S. Infantry, who was killed in action July 1, 1898, at San Juan, Santiago, Cuba.

Situated atop three 50-70 foot high granite outcroppings, Fort Wetherill commanded an unobstructed view of the open sea to the south, with Block Island visible on the horizon and Point Judith in clear sight to the southwest. The view to the east and southeast was obstructed because of the landmass

Preparations for construction of Fort Wetherill, April 1904. Wharf area in foreground with East Passage and Newport beyond.

Photo courtesy Jamestown Historical Society.

on the Newport side of the Bay. The military significance of this strategic spot had been recognized by Rhode Island's earliest colonists, who, during the Revolutionary War, built earthen fortifications above these steep cliffs and installed cannon to protect nearby Newport from the British. Ever since that time the Dumplings-Wetherill area has played an important role in Narragansett Bay defense planning. Permanent fortifications were constructed in 1905-1906.

During the period October-December 1940, when construction of the new barracks and troop facilities had progressed far enough to permit occupancy, elements of the 243rd Coast Artillery Regiment were transferred from Fort Adams across the Bay in order to activate and commence training at four of the seven named Endicott batteries of Fort Wetherill.

Battery 'C' was assigned to the two 3" barbette guns of Battery Crittenden, while the 12" disappearing rifles of Battery Wheaton were manned by members of Battery 'D'. The 12" barbette rifles of Battery Varnum at the easternmost flank of the Wetherill complex were assigned to Battery 'E'. Battery 'F' assumed responsibility for Battery Dickenson and its two 6" shielded rapid-fire rifles.

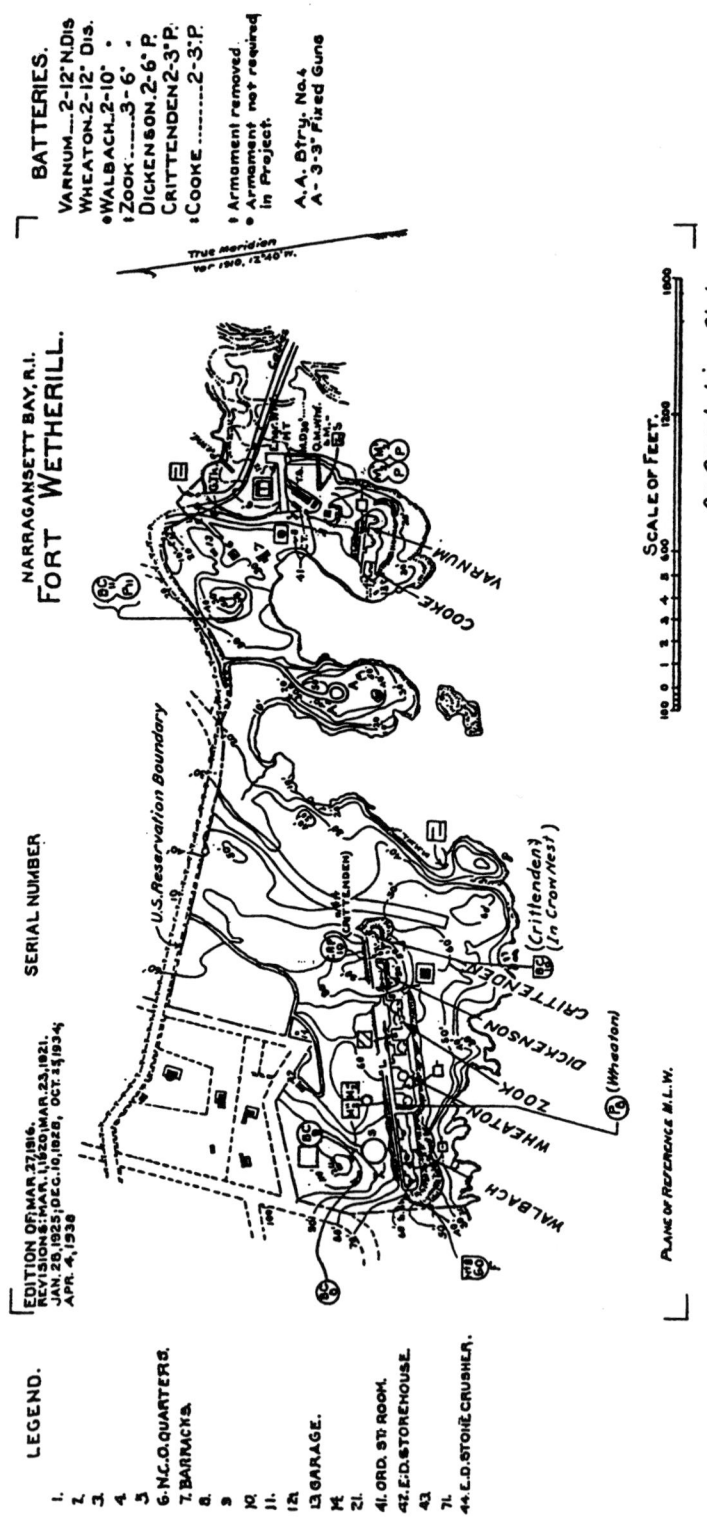

Source: National Archives Record Group 407 (Declassified NND 760162)

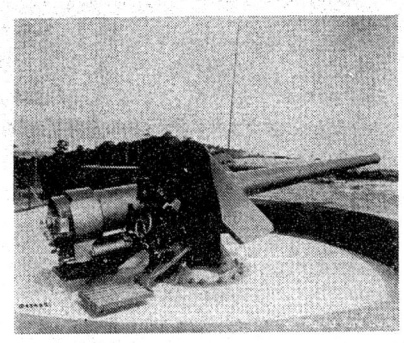 

Left: Six-inch shielded rapid fire guns of the type assigned to Battery Dickenson at Fort Wetherill.

National Archives photo 165-WW-386D-1.

Right: A 12-inch disappearing rifle closely resembling the weapons installed at Battery Wheaton, Fort Wetherill.

Photo courtesy Edward Rowe Snow.

Units of 243rd Coast Artillery Regiment at Fort Wetherill in 1941. Battery Dickenson and members of Battery 'F' of Woonsocket in foreground.

Photo courtesy John C. Rembijas.

Existing 3" fixed antiaircraft guns located on the high cliffs above Sand Beach Cove and West Cove were operated by members of Battery 'G'.

The 10th Coast Artillery, at that time responsible for harbor mining operations, used the QM Wharf at this fort as a base for the Army's mine planter *General Absolom Baird*.

The guns of Batteries Walbach, Zook and Cooke had been removed earlier. Later, several mobile 90mm guns were installed at Fort Wetherill to support mission operations.

The following officers were in command of this fort:

Lt. Col. Frank B. Rhodes, Jr.	243rd C.A. (HD)	Sep. 24, 1940 - Aug. 4, 1942
Major Francis N. Spry	243rd C.A. (HD)	Aug. 4, 1942 - Jan. 28, 1943
Major John R. Dolan	243rd C.A. (HD)	Jan. 28, 1943 - Mar. 1, 1943
Major Francis N. Spry	243rd C.A. (HD)	Mar. 1, 1943 - Jul. 30, 1943
Major Frederick E. Reiber	10th C.A. (HD)	Jul. 30, 1943 - Nov. 4, 1943
Major Robert S. Rumazza		Nov. 4, 1943 - Mar. 10, 1944
Lt. Col. Francis N. Spry	243rd C.A. (HD)	Mar. 10, 1944 - Jul. 27, 1944
Major William McCachern		Jul. 27, 1944 - Aug. 7, 1944
Lt. Col. Francis N. Spry	243rd/188th C.A.	Aug. 7, 1944 - Apr. 18, 1945
Major William McCachern		Apr. 18, 1945 - May 3, 1945
Lt. Col. Francis N. Spry		May 3, 1945 - May 10, 1945
Major William McCachern		May 10, 1945 - Unknown

Army mine planter *General Absolom Baird* **was assigned to the harbor defenses of Narragansett Bay.**

U. S. Army photo SC 134276.

Fort Wetherill in 1974. Road network in former barracks area can be seen in upper portion of photo.

Photo by A. K. Schroeder, CAMP.

The World War II Regimental Chapel at Fort Wetherill was also known as Building T-112.

National Archives photo, RG-77.

Battery Dickenson under camouflage netting 1942-1943.

Photo courtesy J. C. Rembijas.

Fort Getty

Located on a peninsula known as Fox Hill, on the western shore of Conanicut Island, this 31-acre tract of land was acquired by the Government in 1900. Construction of permanent fortifications began in August 1901. Also referred to as Beaverhead, this tract and the adjacent land to the south along the shore were utilized in revolutionary days by the colonists and by the British to control ship movements through the West Passage.

On May 25, 1903, the reservation was named in honor of Colonel George W. Getty, 4th U.S. Artillery, Brevet Major General, U.S. Volunteers, who served with distinction during the Mexican and Civil Wars.

This Endicott-period fort was located approximately one and one-half miles across the water from the batteries of Fort Kearney on the mainland, and one-half mile southeast of Fort Greble on Dutch Island. A garrison was first established at this site in July 1909.

Officers Quarters, Building T-31, in August 1941.
National Archives photo, RG-77.

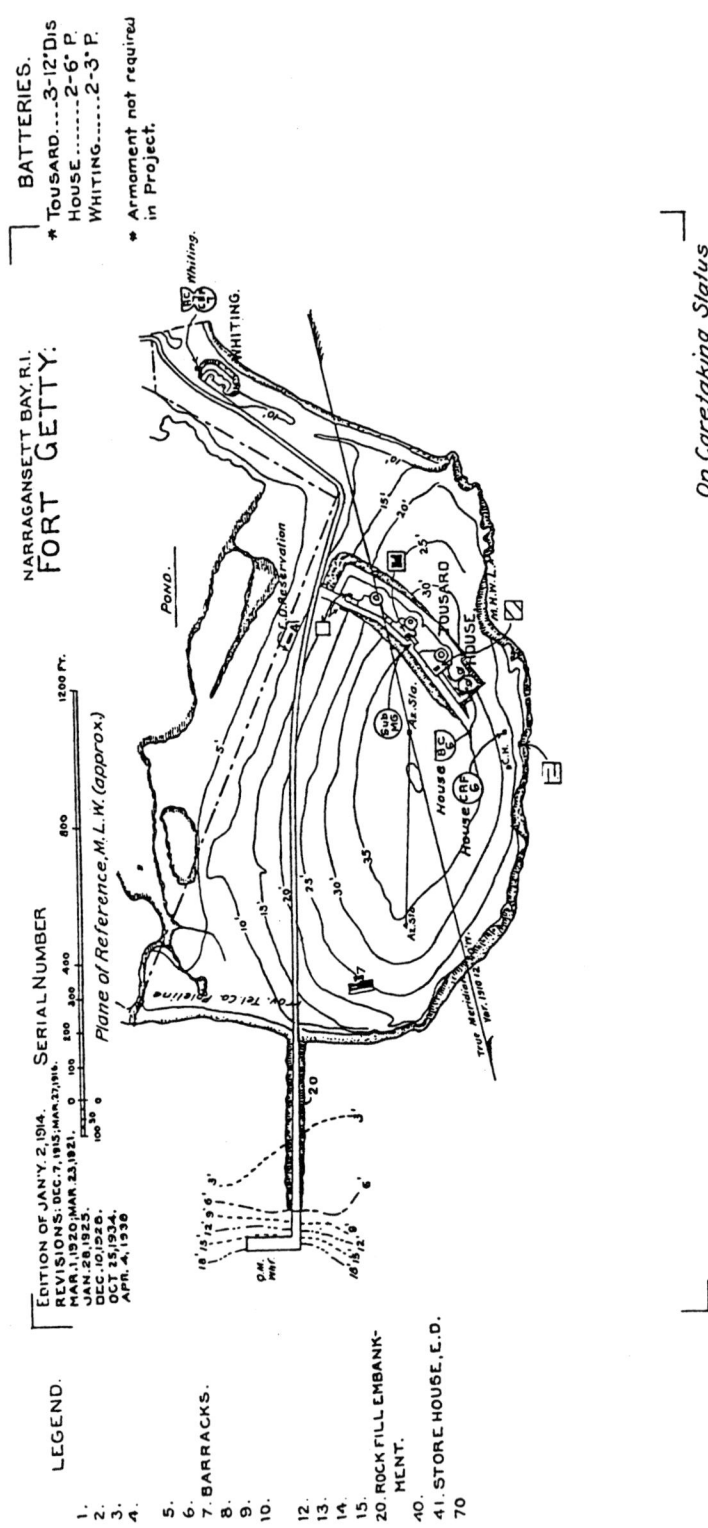

Designated units of the 243rd Coast Artillery left their tents at Fort Adams in late 1940 to be quartered in the new barracks which had been under construction at Fort Getty for several months. The Regiment at that time established its headquarters at the fort, set up a regimental motor pool, and assigned the Medical Detachment and the Band to this site. Personnel of Batteries 'A' and 'B' were included in the transfer to Getty, with Battery 'A' being assigned initially to the 6" barbette guns of Battery House and Battery 'B' to the 3" guns of Battery Whiting, a smaller emplacement at the entrance to the reservation. The searchlight unit, Battery 'K', was also moved to Fort Getty and quickly deployed smaller detachments to strategic sites in the Bay area where searchlights were set up. In 1942, the two 3" guns of Battery Whiting were moved to Fort Burnside and replaced in August 1943 with two 3" rifles from Fort Varnum. These latter armaments originated from Battery Armistead at Fort Kearney.

The 6" rifles of Battery House were moved to Fort Varnum in 1943. In August of that year the three 12" disappearing guns of Battery Toussard were dismantled and removed from Fort Getty. Several gunblocks were later installed to the west of the fortifications to serve as fixed emplacements for 90mm weapons assigned to an anti-motor torpedo boat battery.

The following officers were in command of this fort:

Lt. Col. Ernest W. Moore	243rd C.A. (HD)	Oct. 14, 1940 - Mar. 14, 1941
Col. Earl C. Webster	243rd C.A. (HD)	Mar. 15, 1941 - Dec. 3, 1941
Lt. Col. John F. Datson	243rd C.A. (HD)	Dec. 4, 1941 - Jun. 21, 1942
Col. John F. Datson	243rd C.A. (HD)	Jun. 22, 1942 - Feb. 8, 1944
Col. Russell T. George	243rd C.A. (HD)	Feb. 9, 1944 - Unknown

Left: Guard House, Building T-37, in August 1941. Right: Post Exchange, Building T-36.

National Archives photos, RG-77.

Fort Getty in the 1950's.

Photo courtesy Catharine M. Wright.

Fort Getty, 1974: Landfill operations underway at foot of former Batteries Tousard and House.

Photo by A. K. Schroeder, CAMP.

The burial of Fort Getty in 1979.

Photos by author.

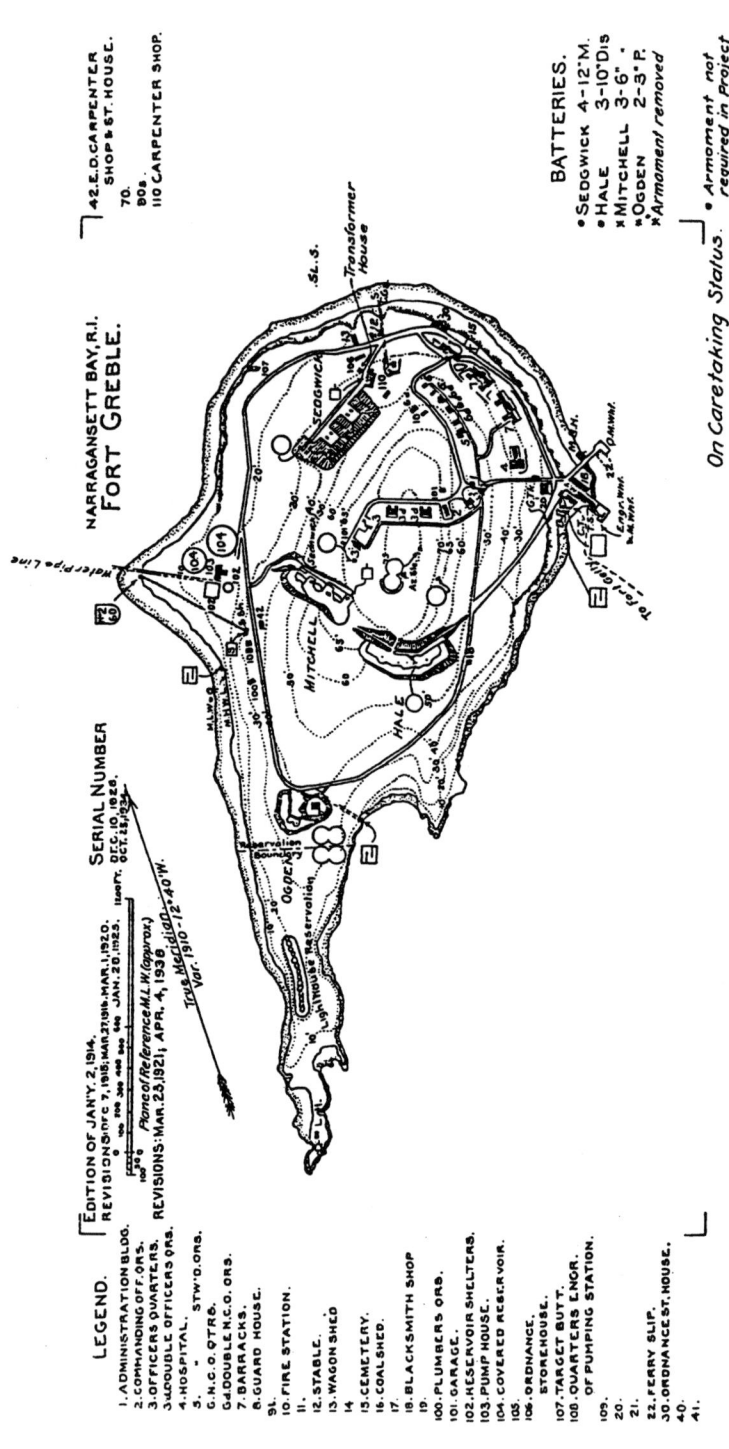

Fort Greble

Situated in the West Passage of Narragansett Bay about one mile west of Conanicut Island, this reservation of 75 acres, acquired in 1864, comprised the total area of Dutch Island except for six acres at the southern end purchased earlier for lighthouse purposes. The island was initially garrisoned for a period of two years by volunteers from Rhode Island. Although small fortifications and temporary buildings were constructed, there was little activity until 1898 when, in the face of the Spanish-American War, the Fort was rebuilt into a modern formidible stronghold including a battery of heavy mortars.

Originally referred to as "the post on Dutch Island," the reservation was given its official name on May 31, 1898, in honor of First Lieutenant John T. Greble, 2nd Artillery, who was the first officer of the Regular Army killed in action in the Civil War. He was born in Philadelphia on January 9, 1834, and fell at Big Bethel, Virginia, on June 10, 1861.

Wharf area at Fort Greble before deactivation of the Dutch Island facility.

Courtesy Jamestown Historical Society.

The facility was deactivated in 1906 and placed in a caretaking status. Well maintained in the intervening years, Fort Greble was again activated in World War I and once again played an important role in the harbor defenses of Narragansett Bay. Several years after that war it was phased down, finally to succumb to the status of a rifle range in the 1940's.

The armaments of batteries Ogden and Mitchell had previously been removed as nonessential, while the 12" mortars of Battery Sedgewick and the guns of Battery Hale were earmarked by the Army for "salvage" due to obsolescence and damage. It may be surmised that the inadequate water supply on Dutch Island limited the use of the island. When garrisoned, water had been piped to cisterns on the island from another Government reservation in Saunderstown. The post was finally discontinued in December 1947.

Dutch Island and Fort Greble in 1974.

Photo by A. K. Schroeder, CAMP.

346th Company in training at Fort Greble in 1922.
Courtesy Jamestown Historical Society.

A 1948 view of Fort Greble structures.
Courtesy R. I. Port Authority.

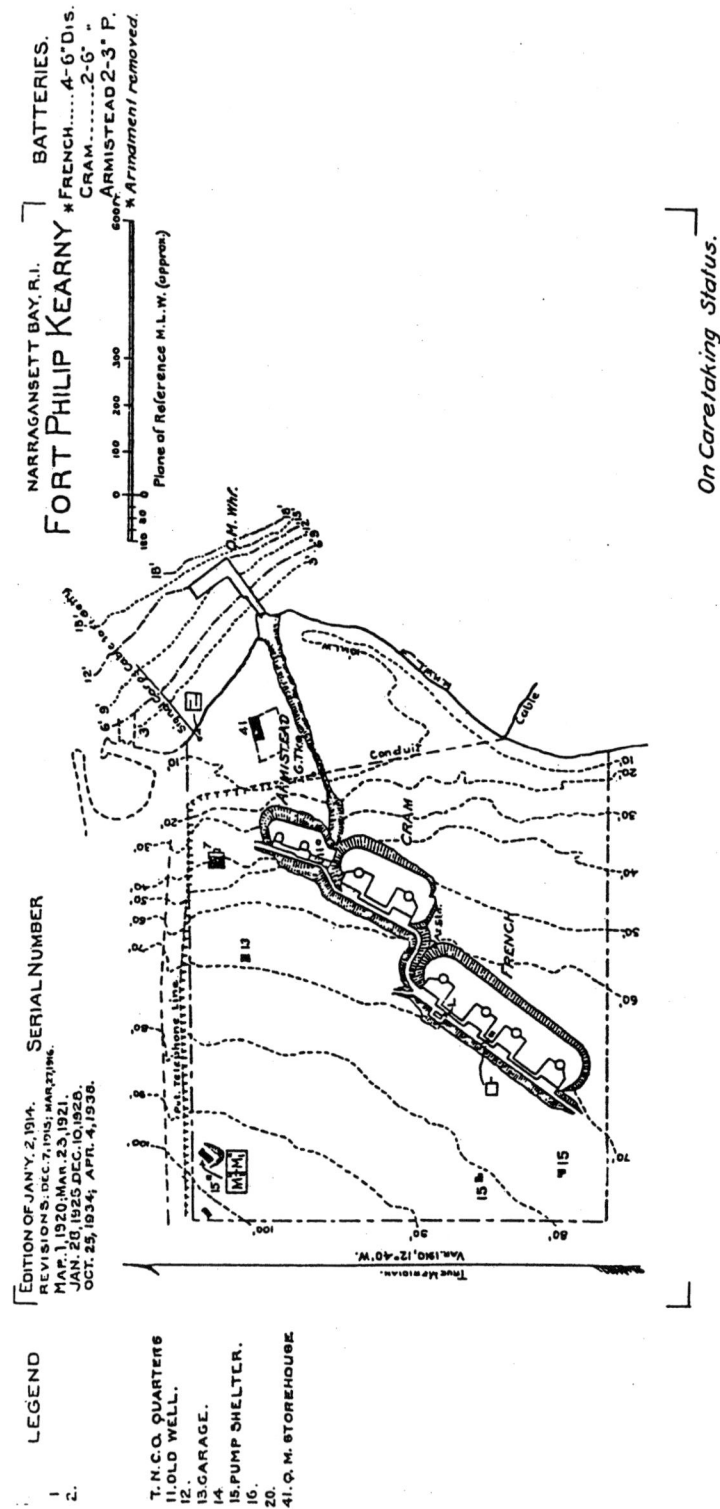

Source: National Archives Record Group 407 (Declassified NND 760162)

Fort Kearney

This 25-acre military reservation, situated near the South Ferry Landing in Saunderstown, was acquired by the Government on May 23, 1901. It was located at the site of a former seaport village established about 1695 and active through the Civil War. On December 27, 1904, the area was named in honor of Major General Phillip Kearney, U.S. Volunteers.

Construction of permanent fortifications at this site began in 1906. This mainland facility was located one and one-half miles due west of Fort Getty on Conanicut Island and about one-half mile southwest of Fort Greble on Dutch Island.

Fort Kearney after completion of construction in 1941.
National Archives photo, RG-77.

A permanent garrison was established here on May 8, 1908. The reservation was manned during World War I and thereafter kept in a caretaking status until reactivated in early 1941. Except for an old stone dwelling dating from 1845, a few pump shelters, a garage, and a storehouse, the reservation was bare. The guns of Battery French had been removed as a result of earlier military reassessments; however, the two 6" disappearing rifles of Battery Cram and the two 3" barbette guns of Battery Armistead were still on site.

A major construction program similar to those initiated at Forts Wetherill and Getty was underway at this installation by late 1940. New barracks, mess facilities, a recreation building, a day-room, administrative offices and other essential structures were erected on the high ground overlooking the Bay. Elements of the 10th Coast Artillery Regiment, Regular Army, moved on to this post in February 1941 as soon as construction progress permitted troop occupancy.

In 1942 the men of the 10th were replaced by an anti-motor torpedo boat battery of the 243rd Coast Artillery Regiment and company-sized units of the 22nd Quartermaster and 132nd Army Engineer Regiments. At that time the 3" rifles of Battery Armistead were moved to Fort Varnum. Two newly installed 37mm guns were the only heavy weapons maintained in an operational status at this site from 1943 until the end of the war.

1951 aerial view of Fort Kearney area. Fortifications and WW II barracks clearly visible.

NOAA photo 10-19-51-J-5079.

Following is a partial listing of senior officers in command of this post during the World War II period:

Capt. Edward L. Schmidt, Jr.	10th C.A.	Feb. 10, 1941 - Oct. 25, 1941
Capt. Kenneth G. Wickham	10th C.A.	Oct. 26, 1941 - Jun. 21, 1942
Capt. Gomer A. Sweeten	22nd Q.M.	Jun. 22, 1942 - Jul. 4, 1942
Capt. George R. Snyder	132nd Engr	Jul. 4, 1942 - Unknown

The University of Rhode Island has found alternative uses for Battery Armistead.

Photo by author.

Construction of URI Marine Laboratory facilities utilizing existing fortifications.

Photo courtesy URI Library.

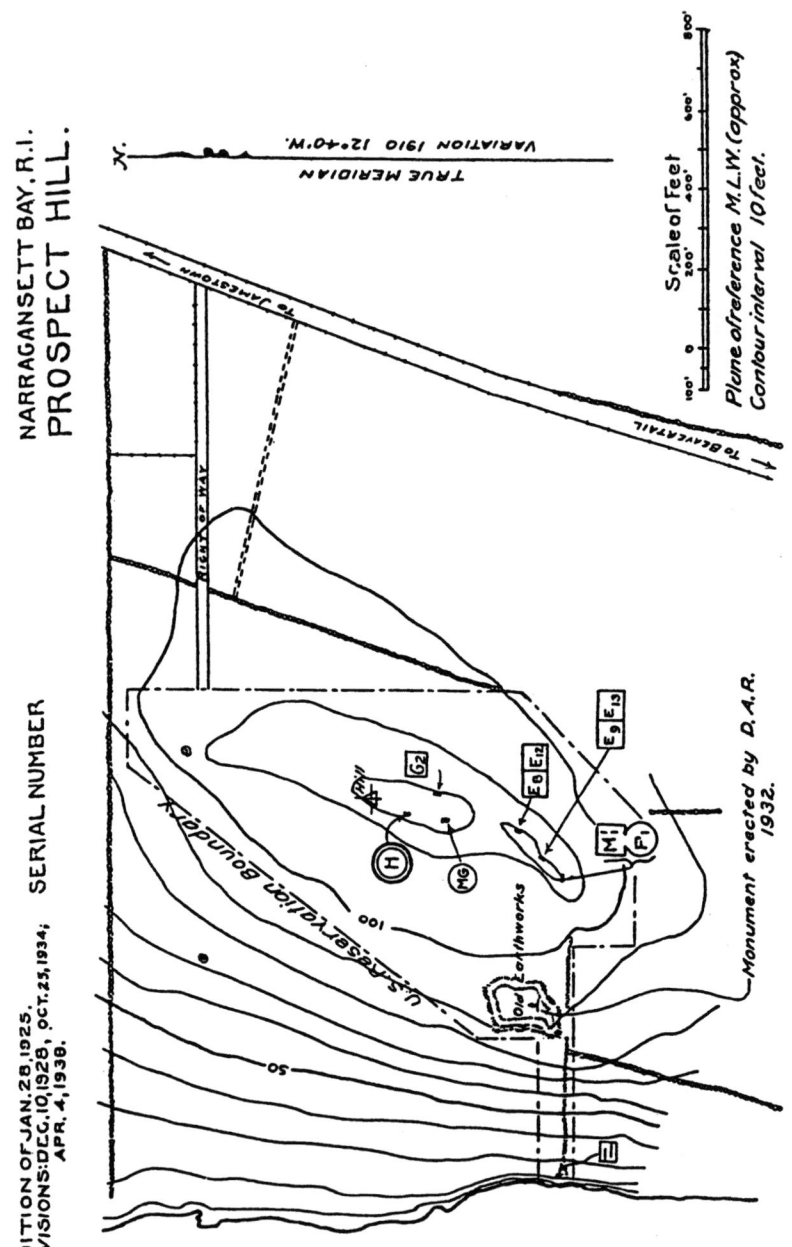

Prospect Hill Fire Control Station

Comprising approximately 18 acres, this reservation was originally acquired by the Government in 1916, with additional land added in 1921. The site, located on the highest ground elevation of Beavertail on Conanicut Island, consisted of six in-ground concrete observation posts. This enclave was in active use in the 1940's, when it served the harbor mining effort as communications link for the operations of Mine Commands 1 and 2 in the East and West Passages of Narragansett Bay. The Mine Command operated a 172' Army mine planter, several 64' craft and a group of 26'-30' mine yawls which were docked at Forts Wetherill and Adams. Fire control points for the mine fields later established were constructed on newly acquired property between Hull Cove and Austin Hollow, on Beavertail. It was along the road in this area that the Army in 1942 established permanent roadblocks to curtail traffic to Fort Burnside and Beavertail Light less than one mile further south.

Located within and near the western perimeter of the Prospect Hill Reservation were Revolutionary earthworks dating back to 1776 and known as Conanicut Battery.

Prospect Hill, Jamestown, site of WW II communications site for harbor defense operations.

Photo courtesy A. K. Schroeder, CAMP.

In-ground observation posts constructed at Prospect Hill, Jamestown, in 1917 were used by the Army during the Second World War.

Photo courtesy A. K. Schroeder, CAMP.

SUPPLY LINES

Transportation between the command post at Fort Adams and units deployed on the west side of the Bay was by ferry to Jamestown on Conanicut Island and from there to Saunderstown via the Jamestown Bridge, which had been opened to traffic on July 27, 1940, just two months before the 243rd had been activated. The Army also operated a boat shuttle service between Fort Kearney on the mainland and the dock at Fort Getty, the seat of the regimental headquarters. Similarly, military shuttle craft were put into operation between Fort Adams in Newport and the docking facilities in Jamestown and Fort Wetherill.

A 155mm field piece being off-loaded from ferry in Newport.

Photo courtesy A. K. Schroeder, CAMP.

PART III

A New Generation of Seacoast Fortifications

THE WORLD WAR II BATTERIES

Engaged in a resurvey of harbor defenses since March 1940, the Army's Harbor Defense Board expanded its study to a complete reassessment of U.S. coastal and harbor defense needs following the downfall of France in June of that year. On July 27, 1940, the Board recommended the construction of twenty-seven 16" gun batteries, each with two guns and a range of approximately 26 miles, at strategic points along the coast. Such construction would meet current military requirements while simultaneously replacing practically all of the existing pre-World War I batteries. The weapons needed for this project were available from a stock of guns previously produced and earmarked for installation on capital ships of the Navy whose construction had been cancelled as a result of the Washington Naval Treaty of 1922.

Sakonnet Point in Little Compton and Point Judith were among the sites recommended for construction of these modern long-range seacoast batteries. The contemplated layout and construction of the gun emplacements represented a radical departure from the fortifications in existence in the Narragansett Bay area at that time. The various shortcomings of the older batteries noted earlier were to be overcome by emplacing the giant-sized rifles in casemates under cover of 20-25 feet of reinforced concrete, steel, and earth and spacing the armaments approximately 500 feet apart. With only their barrels protruding from the casemates, the guns of these batteries were to be connected by a system of adjoining underground concrete chambers housing the ammunition magazines, electrical power generating plants, communica-

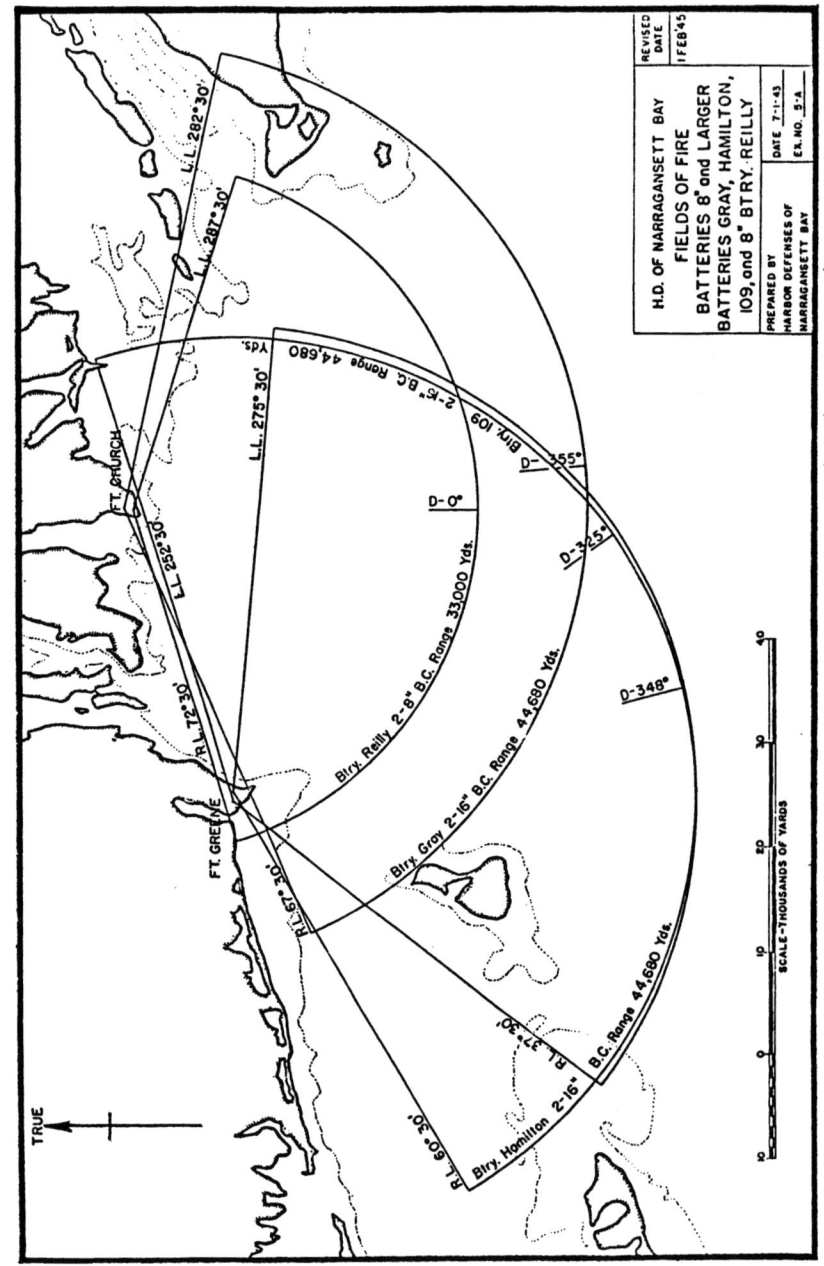

tions facilities and air conditioning systems, and providing the required storage and operating spaces. The shells, which weighed approximately one ton, were to be transported within the subterranean complex by overhead trolleys running on tracks suspended from the ceilings, while thick concrete canopies would protrude outward above the gun ports as added protection against direct hits from naval or aerial bombardment. Massive steel shields were to be installed at the gun portals as further protection against enemy shelling and shrapnel.

A typical 16-inch gun of the type emplaced at strategic points along the coast early in WW II. In 1938 a single gun and carriage was estimated to cost approximately $520,000.

Photo courtesy A. K. Schroeder, CAMP.

Utilization of surplus naval 8" guns for harbor defense purposes was also proposed, with the only casemated battery of this size ultimately constructed near Sakonnet Point.

To provide added capabilities against cruisers and other light ships, the Board also proposed the construction of fifty secondary 6" gun batteries, each with an effective range of 15 miles. Sakonnet Point, Point Judith and Fort Burnside at the southern end of Conanicut Island were among the sites selected for this type of installation in the Narragansett Bay area.

These smaller caliber weapons were envisioned as two-gun batteries which would not be casemated. Instead, the rifles would be located in an exposed position enclosed on three sides and from above by a curved wraparound-type cast steel shield four to six inches in thickness. The two guns of each battery would be spaced about 200 feet apart with an earth-covered concrete magazine structure between them, readily accessible from each of the guns.

As a result of earlier military decisions, construction had commenced at several sites even before the July 1940 recommendations of the Board were published. The latest assessment and proposals served to confirm the need for continuing the ongoing modernization projects while at the same time triggering action for additional construction. The programs progressed rapidly until about one year after the U.S. became actively embroiled in the war as a result of Japan's December 7, 1941, attack on Pearl Harbor and Germany's declaration of war on December 11. The early advances of the Japanese forces demanded serious reallocation of Army and Navy resources to effectively consolidate the American position in the Far East. This shift in priorities required the subordination of the coastal defense modernization program at home. The subsequent turn of events in the war in favor of the United States and its allies in the Pacific as well as in Europe brought about further curtailments in the continental defense program. By mid 1944 the need for coastal and harbor defenses had diminished to the point that further expenditures were no longer necessary.

Fort Church

By War Department General Order No. 5 of May 1, 1940, the military reservation at West Main Road, Little Compton, Rhode Island, until then known as Sakonnet Point Military Reservation, was designated Fort Church. The area was given its name in honor of Colonel Benjamin Church, who was a colonial citizen-soldier and Indian fighter. Born in Plymouth, Massachusetts, in 1639, he distinguished himself in King Philip's War (1675-1679), King William's War (1690-1697) and Queen Anne's War (1702-1704). He founded Little Compton, retired from active service in 1704, and died in 1718. Land acquisition in the Sakonnet Point area for coastal defense purposes had commenced in 1939. The Fort Church complex consisted of three separate parcels known as the North, East, and South Reservations respectively. The garrison was formally established on December 11, 1941, under the command of Major Isidore H. Stern. Troops of the 10th Coast Artillery Regiment were assigned to this facility until February-March 1944, when they were relieved by personnel of the 243rd Coast Artillery Regiment.

The succession of Commanding Officers at Fort Church was as follows:

Lt. Col. Oliver H. Gilbert	Apr. 5, 1942 to Sep. 15, 1942
Major William A. Hinternhoff	Sep. 15, 1942 to Jan. 27, 1943
Major Dean J. Natali	Jan. 27, 1943 to Sep. 28, 1943
Lt. Col. Joseph DeRita	Sep. 28, 1943 to Feb. 4, 1944
Capt. Frederick A. Thompson	Feb. 5, 1944 to Apr. 1, 1945
Capt. Bernard H. Schimmel	Apr. 1, 1945 to May 22, 1945
1st Lt. Sidney P. Gilbert	May 22, 1945 to Jan. 8, 1946

All is quiet now. Postwar view of casemate which sheltered a 16-inch rifle at Fort Church during the war.

Phoenix-Times photo by Bruce Burdett.

NORTH RESERVATION — BATTERY GRAY

This 139-acre tract of land, formerly owned by Daniel Wilbour and members of his family, was selected by the Army for installation of two 16" rifles on barbette carriages emplaced within bombproof and well-camouflaged casemates. The gun battery was given the name Battery Gray in honor of Major Quinn Gray, Coast Artillery Corps, U.S. Army, who died in 1929 after a long and distinguished career as an officer. Construction of the Battery Gray complex commenced on September 21, 1939, with final completion recorded as May 15, 1942. The manning table for this facility called for a complement of 190 men distributed as follows:

16" Gun Crews (2)	85
Plotting Room	25
Battery Command	5
Observation Stations (10 with 4 men each)	40
Caliber .30 Machine Guns (2)	6
Caliber .50 Machine Guns (4)	17
40mm Antiaircraft Guns (2)	12
Total Complement:	190 men

Gate and main corridor of earth-covered Battery Gray complex forty years later.

Phoenix-Times photos by Bruce Burdett.

The two guns of this battery were located 500 feet apart within an earth-covered complex which embraced approximately 33,500 cubic feet of space. Movement of the shells from the 12,240 cubic foot magazine was via one and one-half ton army-type trolley hoists which travelled on 7" ceiling-suspended "I" beams within the complex for a distance of about 300 feet to reach either of the two guns.

Both weapons installed were of the Mark II Model M1 type, mounted on a Model 1919M1 barbette-type carriage. Maximum elevation of these rifles was 46°. Gay Head on Martha's Vineyard, the island of No Mans Land, as well as the southernmost island in the Elizabeth Island chain were all well within the 26-mile range of Battery Gray.

Ten fire control points served this battery. They were located at Green Hill, Point Judith, Fort Varnum, Sachuest Point, Fort Church, Warren Point, Gooseberry Neck, Cuttyhunk, Gay Head, and Block Island. A seacoast radar at Brenton Point also serviced this battery. Barracks and related facilities were erected at this reservation.

EAST RESERVATION — BATTERY REILLY

The East Reservation, formerly owned by Harry Richmond, was the selected site for installation of two 8" seacoast guns. These rifles were emplaced in earth-covered concrete casements similar in design and construction to Battery Gray except somewhat smaller. The total space taken up by this underground complex was approximately 11,640 cubic feet, with about one-third of that space devoted to shell storage. This battery was given the name Battery Reilly in honor of Henry Joseph Reilly, a native of Ireland who joined the Army as a private in 1866 and became a Captain on January 3, 1894. He was killed in action at Peking, China, on August 15, 1900.

Construction of Battery Reilly commenced in early June 1940, with final completion recorded as January 5, 1942.

This facility required a military complement of 129 men as follows:

8" Gun Crews (2)	53
Plotting Room	20
Battery Command	5
Observation Stations (6 with 4 men each)	24
Caliber .30 Machine Guns (2)	6
Caliber .50 Machine Guns (2)	9
40mm Antiaircraft Guns (2)	12
Total Complement:	129 men

Half-ton trolleys supported on 5" "I" beam rails were utilized to move shells to the guns, which were roughly 150 feet in either direction from the magazine. The 18-mile range of these guns provided the battery with a capability to engage shipping within an arc roughly commencing at Fort Greene (South) to the west and Gay Head to the east. The weapons were of the Navy Mark VI, Model 3A2 type and mounted on 8" Model M1 barbette carriages.

Fire control points for this battery were established at Fort Greene, Fort Varnum, Sachuest Point, Warren Point, Gooseberry Neck, and Cuttyhunk. A radar installation at Sachuest Point was linked to this battery. The East Reservation included housing for troops, a theater, a fire station and a supply operation.

8-inch emplacement of Battery Reilly, Little Compton, Rhode Island in 1980.

Phoenix-Times photo by Bruce Burdett.

SOUTH RESERVATION — BATTERY 212

Situated at Sakonnet Point, this enclave comprised about 21 acres of land originally owned by Dr. Henry D. Lloyd. Two 6" barbette-mounted rapid-fire rifles designated Battery 212 were installed at this site. Construction of this battery commenced on November 10, 1941, with final completion recorded as August 6, 1943. Both weapons were of the Model 1903 A2 type mounted on M1 barbette carriages. Unlike the guns of batteries Gray and Reilly, the guns of Battery 212 were not casemated but were protected by a wraparound-type steel shield about 5" thick. These rifles were set on concrete gunblocks allowing for a complete 360° traverse. The ammunition magazine was situated between and slightly to the rear of the two guns in an earth-covered bombproof shelter 9,775 cubic feet in size. Hoists were not installed in this magazine. The 15-mile range of this battery was far superior to the 9-mile range of the older 6" guns of Batteries Dickenson at Fort Wetherill and House at Fort Getty, and later at Fort Varnum.

Operation of Battery 212 required a complement of 123 personnel deployed as follows:

6" Gun Crews (2)	54
Plotting Room	13
Battery Command	5
Observation Stations (6 with 4 men each)	24
Caliber .30 Machine Guns (2)	6
Caliber .50 Machine Guns (2)	9
40mm Antiaircraft Guns (2)	12
Total Complement:	123 men

Typical WW II six-inch gun installation with Navy turret.
Photo in collection of Gerald W. Butler, Captain, MSG, trustee.

A 1954 view of South Reservation and Battery 212, Fort Church.
Photo in author's collection.

Battery 212 maintained fire control points at Point Judith, Fort Varnum, Sachuest Point, Warren Point, Gooseberry Neck and Cuttyhunk. A seacoast radar at Warren Point also serviced this battery.

During the period December 11, 1941, to August 20, 1943, two 155mm Model 1918 field pieces were assigned and emplaced at the Sakonnet Point reservation.

Mobile 155mm guns were temporarily emplaced at critical points along the shore pending construction of permanent fortifications.

Photo in collection of Gerald W. Butler, Captain, MSG, trustee.

Fort Greene

In General Order No. 10 of September 10, 1941, the War Department announced the establishment of the military reservation located at Point Judith, Narragansett, Rhode Island, as a permanent military post. The facility was designated Fort Nathanael Greene in honor of General Nathanael Greene, who was born at Potowomut, Rhode Island, in 1742. The son of a Quaker preacher, Greene was a self-educated man who entered the Rhode Island Assembly in 1770 and played an active role in planning to resist the British Government with force. In 1775 he was appointed Brigadier General and served in command of Rhode Island troops in Boston. As a Major General he was placed in charge of Continental forces on Long Island in 1776. General Greene had a distinguished military career, participating with distinction in military engagements at Harlem Heights, Trenton, Princeton, Brandywine and Germantown. In 1778 he became Quartermaster General and in 1780 took command of the Army of the South. He suffered setbacks in the battles of Guilford Courthouse, Hookirks Hill, South Carolina, and at Eutaw Springs. Troops under his command eventually drove the British from Georgia and the Carolinas. After the war in 1785 General Greene moved to Georgia, where he died in 1786.

The construction of Fort Greene. Battery Hamilton (16-inch) in foreground. Work progressing on Battery 109 across road above.

National Archives photo, RG-338.

Proceedings to acquire the Point Judith military reservation for coastal defense purposes got underway in 1939. Similar to Fort Church in Little Compton, this World War II defense site consisted of three separate areas known as the East, West and South Reservations. Captain Frederick O. Roever, 243rd Coast Artillery Regiment, was the first Commanding Officer of this post. He assumed command on April 15, 1943.

He was later succeeded as follows:

Major Thomas L. Fortin	243rd C.A. (HD)	May 28, 1943 to Jul. 30, 1943
Major Francis N. Spry	243rd C.A. (HD)	Jul. 31, 1943 to Sep. 23, 1943
Lt. Col. Francis N. Spry	243rd C.A. (HD)	Sep. 24, 1943 to Mar. 11, 1944
Capt. John C. Rembijas	243rd C.A. (HD)	Mar. 12, 1944 to Sep. 30, 1944
Capt. John C. Rembijas	188th C.A. Bn (HD)	Oct. 1, 1944 to Apr. 10, 1945
Capt. George Forstot		Apr. 10, 1945 to May 21, 1945
1st Lt. William E. Stetson		May 21, 1945 to Unknown

On July 24, 1943, Headquarters Second Battalion, 243rd C. A. Regiment, moved from Fort Wetherill to Fort Greene.

EAST RESERVATION — BATTERY HAMILTON

This reservation comprised roughly 145 acres of land which became the site of a two-gun 16" battery, mounted on barbette carriages and protected by a concrete- and earth-covered casemate similar in design to Battery Gray at Fort Church. Construction at the East Reservation commenced during the month of September 1940, with the project initially known as Battery 108. In accordance with War Department Order No. 13 of September 24, 1941, the project was given the name Battery Hamilton in honor of Brigadier General Alston Hamilton, U.S. Army, who was born in Oxford, North Carolina, on October 20, 1871, and who graduated from the U.S. Military Academy in 1894 and the Army War College in 1914. General Hamilton served in the Spanish-American War and later in his career held command positions in various coast artillery units, which included service in France during World War I with the 35th Coast Artillery Brigade. He was also the Commanding Officer of the Panama Canal Coast Artillery District from 1919-1921. He retired in 1935 after a long and eventful military career.

Installed at this site were Model 1919 naval barrels with one rifle of the Mark 2 and the other of the Mark 3 type. Both were mounted on Army carriages. Two projectile rooms formed part of the underground complex, each capable of

One of the two 16-inch guns of Battery Hamilton as seen in November 1943.

National Archives photo, RG-338.

Battery Hamilton looked much like other 16-inch gun installations along the East Coast. Here, Battery Murphy, at East Point, Nahant, Massachusetts.

Photo in collection of Gerald W. Butler, Captain, MSG, trustee.

storing 100 rounds of ammunition. Individual projectiles weighing 2,240 lbs. were moved via overhead trolleys. The two powder rooms were sufficient in size to allow storing 600 cases or 100 full charges of powder in each of the chambers.

In February 1943, a detachment of 30 men from Battery 'E' of the 243rd Coast Artillery Regiment was assigned to Battery Hamilton, with the unit reaching full strength at this site by April 15, 1943. Secondary weapons allocated to the battery included four 37mm guns and four .50 caliber and two .30 caliber machine guns. The 37mm guns were later replaced with 40mm weapons. Twelve base end stations serviced this battery as well as three radar installations, one of which was manned by members of 'E' battery at Point Judith.

Three practice rounds were fired by Battery Hamilton on August 6, 1943.

WEST RESERVATION — BATTERY 109

Approximately 90 acres comprised the West Reservation of Fort Greene. Selected as the site of a second two-gun 16" battery within the area of this post, construction never progressed to a point of final completion. An aerial photograph taken on November 2, 1943, shows the rifles of Battery Hamilton on the East Reservation protruding from their

Casemate of Battery 109 (16-inch) at Fort Greene.

Photo by author.

Command Post, Battery 109.

Photo by author.

casemates while the concrete skeletal structure of Battery 109 nearby was still without earth cover. Battery 109 was one of several along the East Coast whose construction was suspended by the War Department during the latter part of 1943.

A concrete silo was constructed on the West Reservation as part of a group of farm buildings, with the silo designed to function as a battery command post.

SOUTH RESERVATION — BATTERY 211

Located adjacent to the Point Judith lighthouse, this 34-acre enclave became the site of a two-gun 6" battery installation known as Battery 211. Both weapons were Model 1903A2 armaments mounted on Army M1 barbette carriages and protected by naval turrets. Construction at this site commenced in December 1941, with members of Battery 'F', 243rd Coast Artillery Regiment, transferring to this location from Fort Wetherill on July 23, 1943. 600 rounds of ammunition and necessary powder charges were stored for each of the weapons in an earth-covered concrete magazine located between the two gun emplacements. Secondary armaments assigned to this battery consisted of two 37mm guns, two .50 caliber machine guns on M3 mounts, plus two .30 caliber machine guns. The 37mm mobile weapons were replaced

Fort Greene — South. Six-inch gun emplacement No. 211 at left. Three base end stations camouflaged to appear as cottages can be seen at the right.

Photo courtesy U. S. Army Corps of Engineers.

The remains of the base end stations at Fort Greene-South in 1979.

Photo by author.

with 40mm guns on April 17, 1944. Near the site of Battery 211, four Panama-type gun emplacements had been constructed earlier to allow for installation of 155mm field artillery pieces as an interim measure. These guns had a 15-mile range. The gun mounts were essentially circular concrete platforms with steel rails around the rims, along which the guns' trails could easily be moved, allowing for full 360° traverse of a field piece around its own vertical axis.

The South Reservation was the site of several fire control points, referred to as "base end stations." These were concrete structures used as observation posts which had been given a wooden facade to provide the appearance of residential cottages. To the north of the gun emplacements barracks had been erected for troop housing and support. Six off-site base end stations provided battery 211 with the required observation capability. A radar installation at Green Hill Beach was tied into the fire control system of this battery.

Fort Burnside — Beavertail

This Fort was located at Beavertail Point, the extreme southern tip of Conanicut Island. As the most seaward promontory of the Beavertail peninsula and one of the most exposed headlands in the Narragansett Bay area, the fort at Beavertail Point was surrounded by open ocean on three sides. The area's significance dates back to 1749, when the third of only seven East Coast lighthouses built before the Revolutionary War was placed on its headland. The present lighthouse was built in 1856 and is the most recent of an unbroken line of lighthouses that has occupied the site.

An area of 118 acres to the north of the lighthouse was taken over by the Government in August 1942 and named Fort Burnside on December 4, in honor of Major General Ambrose E. Burnside, U.S. Army. Born at Liberty, Indiana, on May 23, 1824, General Burnside graduated from West Point in 1847 but resigned from the Army in 1852 to become Major General of the Volunteer Militia in Rhode Island. In 1861, he organized the First Rhode Island Regiment. He led the charge at Bull Run and commanded the Army of the Potomac later in the Civil War. He invented the breech-loading carbine and became a prominent industrialist in Providence after the war. General Burnside served the State of Rhode Island as Governor from 1866 to 1868. He died on September 13, 1881.

The following officers were in command of this fort:

Capt. James A. Ward	Dec. 22, 1942 to Jan. 19, 1943
1st Lt. Harold E. Bridge	Jan. 20, 1943 to May 31, 1943
Lt. Col. I. Henry Stern	Jun. 1, 1943 to Sep. 30, 1944
Major Robert S. P. Rumazza	Oct. 1, 1944 to Jun. 30, 1945
Capt. John C. Rembijas	Jun 30, 1945 to Unknown

Beavertail Light Station in August 1944. A searchlight is installed in front of the lighthouse.

Photo courtesy U. S. Coast Guard.

BATTERY 213

Fort Burnside was one of three sites in the Narragansett Bay area selected for construction of modern two-gun 6" batteries. The new facility, given the designation Battery 213, consisted of two fully steel-shielded guns on barbette carriages which were emplaced on concrete pads in an open field 200 feet apart. Between these was located a bombproof and earth-covered concrete reinforced structure which housed powder and shell rooms, spotting and plotting rooms, air compressors, motor generators, and storage areas. Each gun crew maintained its own allocation of powder and shells within the complex while sharing the plotting and spotting room facilities. There were two entrances to the bunker, allowing for ease of access from either gun position. Five off-site fire control points and a radar serviced this weapons installation.

Battery 213 (6-inch) at Fort Burnside. Beavertail lighthouse in rear.
U. S. Army Military History Institute photo.

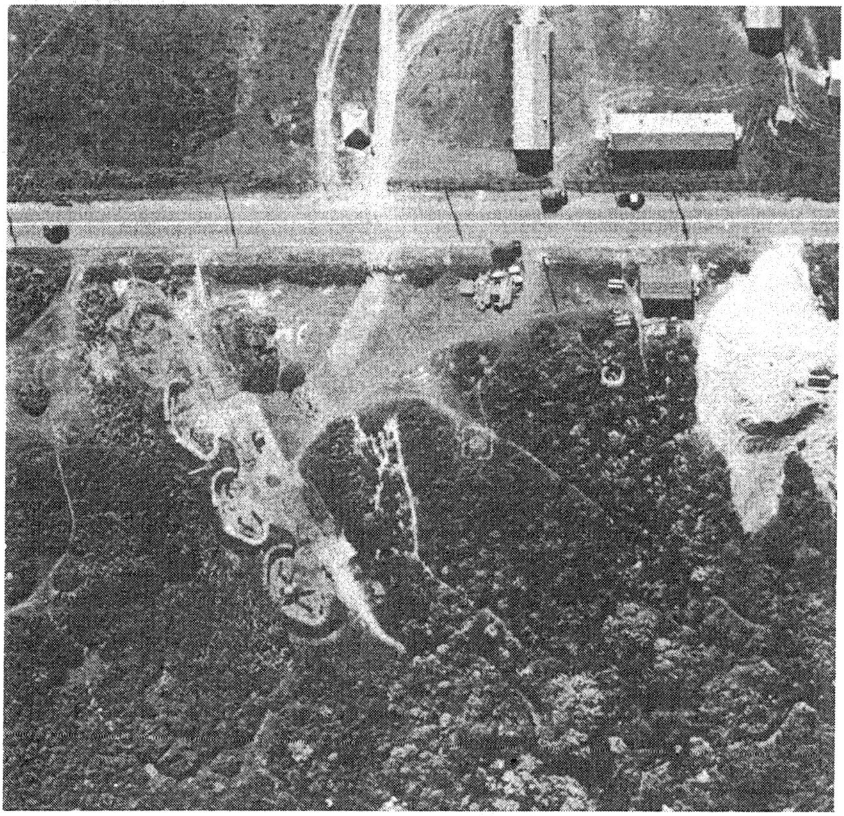

In this aerial photograph of June 13, 1942, several emplacements for mobile artillery pieces can be seen within the Fort Burnside reservation.
National Archives photo, RG-338.

3" BATTERY WHITING

Relocation of Battery Whiting from Fort Getty to Fort Burnside took place during the summer of 1942 after construction of a new magazine and gun platforms for the 3" guns was completed. The battery was sited on the eastern perimeter of the enclave facing Brenton Point across the Bay. The weapons were emplaced on concrete gun blocks 100 feet apart and partially protected by a circular embankment of earth thrown up around each. To the rear and in the center of these positions, a small magazine and a battery command facility were constructed of concrete and covered with earth. This structure had one entrance only, which faced west, away from the guns. Battery Whiting was assigned to guard and protect the mines which had been planted in the East Passage.

Beavertail 1979: Clues to the past.

Photo by author.

HARBOR ENTRANCE CONTROL POST

Even before the Army acquired the addtional land at Beavertail in August 1942, a joint Army-Navy Harbor Entrance Control Post had been established near the Coast Guard operated lighthouse in July 1941. This post was responsible to the Harbor Defense Commander at Fort Adams to report and identify all ships approaching or seeking entry into Narragansett Bay. The examination area for the Harbor Entrance Control Post was defined as south of an east-west line through Brenton Reef Lightship and east of a north-south line through Beavertail Light. In the early days following the activation of the Harbor Entrance Control Post, the unit was housed in a two-room 12' x 30' wooden observation shack erected between the ocean beach and the lighthouse. A few months later, a second small observation post was built just north of the light to command the entrance into the West Passage. The assigned naval officers and men were at that time quartered at Fort Getty with members of the 243rd Coast Artillery Regiment. The temporary operating spaces at Beavertail were abandoned on July 1, 1943, when the Harbor Entrance Control Post moved into permanent quarters in the Army-constructed Cottage C-1, a two-story structure outfitted with loop and underwater sound detection equipment, radar, radio, visual signalling facilities and spaces for the Officer-in-Charge, duty officers and enlisted personnel. A bridge, equipped with 12- and 24-inch searchlights, commanded an unobstructed view to the east, west and south.

In this photo of June 1942, the original Harbor Entrance Control Post can be seen in front of the lighthouse. Battery Whiting (3-inch) under construction.

National Archives photo, RG-338.

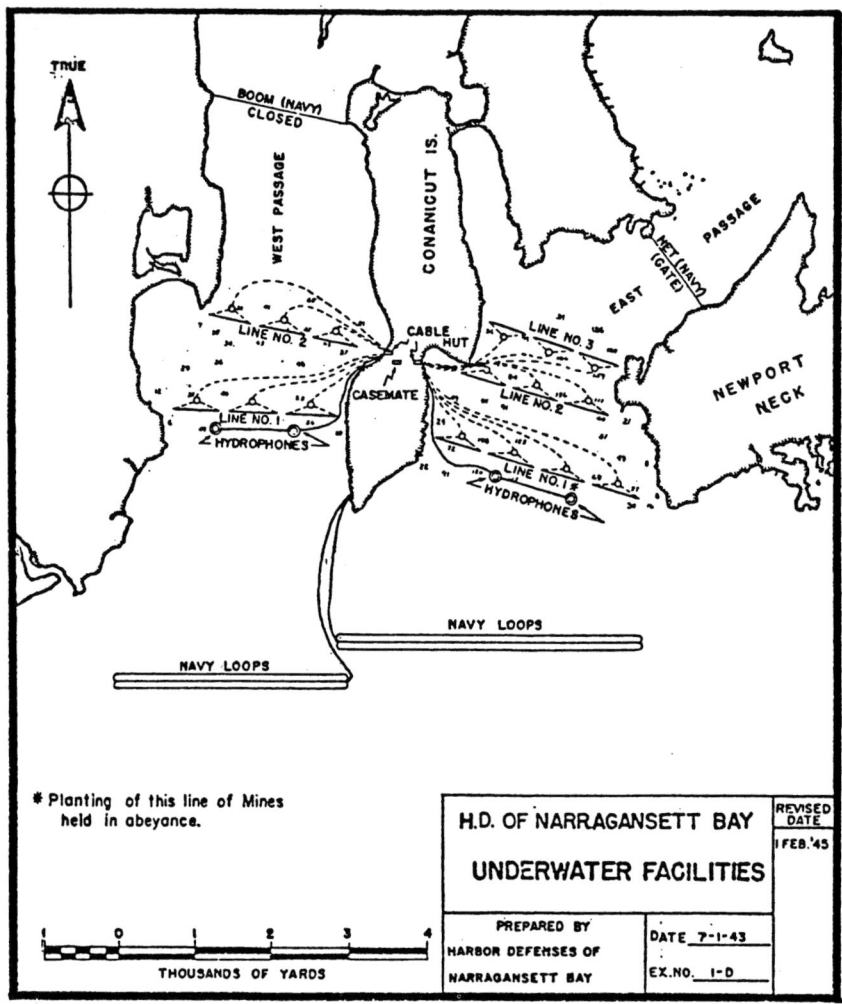

Source: National Archives Record Group 407 (Declassified)

In early 1942, two Navy submarine detector loops consisting of 90,000 feet of magnetic cable were laid in the waters a few miles south of the Harbor Entrance Control Post. The loops were connected to a receiving station at the Harbor Entrance Control Post until July 16, 1944, when this detection system was removed. On February 2, 1942, the Navy installed an antisubmarine net with gate in the East Passage, extending southeast across the channel from Fort Wetherill. A second antisubmarine net, but without a gate, was suspended from an antiboat boom placed across the West Passage from Fort Kearney to Fort Getty. On February 10, 1942, the West Passage and the Sakonnet River were closed to all but specially licensed traffic. Both nets and the boom were removed in September 1944.

The largest naval complement assigned to the Harbor Entrance Control Post at any one time was in the summer of 1943, when unit strength totalled nine officers and 40 enlisted men.

The Harbor Entrance Control Post was disestablished at midnight of June 27, 1945. The facility commenced operations as the Beavertail Signal Station one minute later.

An antiboat boom suspended between Fort Kearney (foreground) and Fort Getty (across water) served to block the West Passage to all vessels.

National Archives photo 80-G-452545.

In this World War II photo, Battery Dickenson is under camouflage at Fort Wetherill (right), while a large Navy ship is preparing to pass through the gate in the antiboat net and boom suspended across the East Passage.

Photo courtesy J. C. Rembijas.

East Passage, June 18, 1943. Navy gate tenders service antisubmarine net and antiboat defenses. Fort Wetherill in distance.

National Archives photo 80-G-452348.

Beavertail Communications Station from a painting by Mrs. Catharine M. Wright.

Photo by author.

Fort Varnum

In February 1942 the War Department approved the acquisition of 33 acres of waterfront property off Boston Neck Road for another military reservation. Construction of a complete Army camp including barracks, mess hall and other required facilities was started on April 23, 1942, and a garrison was established on August 5. On April 18, 1943, the new post was dedicated in honor of General James Mitchell Varnum, born in Dracut, Massachusetts, in 1748. He attended Harvard University and Rhode Island College (now Brown University), from which he graduated with honors in 1769. He became a student of law, was admitted to the Rhode Island Bar in 1771, and settled in East Greenwich, where he became a charter member and an officer of the Kentish Guards in 1774. He was commissioned Brigadier General of the State Militia in 1776 after participating in the defense of Boston, and in 1777 accepted an appointment at the same rank in the Continental Army, leading his men admirably during the critical winter months at Valley Forge. In 1778 General Varnum played an important role in the Battle of Rhode Island. Returning to the practice of law in 1779, he later became a judge for the Northwest Territory. An outstanding soldier, an accomplished scholar, and a brilliant orator, he died at age 40 in Marietta, Ohio, in 1789.

Two gunblocks were constructed near the water's edge to receive the older 6" rapid fire rifles of Battery House, until then located at Fort Getty. A battery command post and earth-covered magazine structure were also installed nearby. Additional gunblocks were poured in the same area for the fixed installation of 90mm and 37mm guns required for antimotor torpedo boat operations. This cluster of weapons was known as Battery 921. A dual searchlight with on-site radar support was also located at this post. Two 3" weapons were temporarily installed at this site and relocated to Fort Getty in August 1943.

Several fire control points of concrete, camouflaged to resemble private dwellings, dotted the compound. From these points aiming data was transmitted to the 16" gun battery at Fort Greene, the 8" and 16" guns at Fort Church, and all the 6" weapons of Batteries 211, 212, 213, as well as those of Battery Dickenson at Fort Wetherill.

On December 31, 1943, Batteries 'A' and 'C' of the 243rd Coast Artillery Regiment were assigned to this site. Frequent movement of troops to and from Fort Varnum eventually also brought members of the 10th Coast Artillery Regiment to this

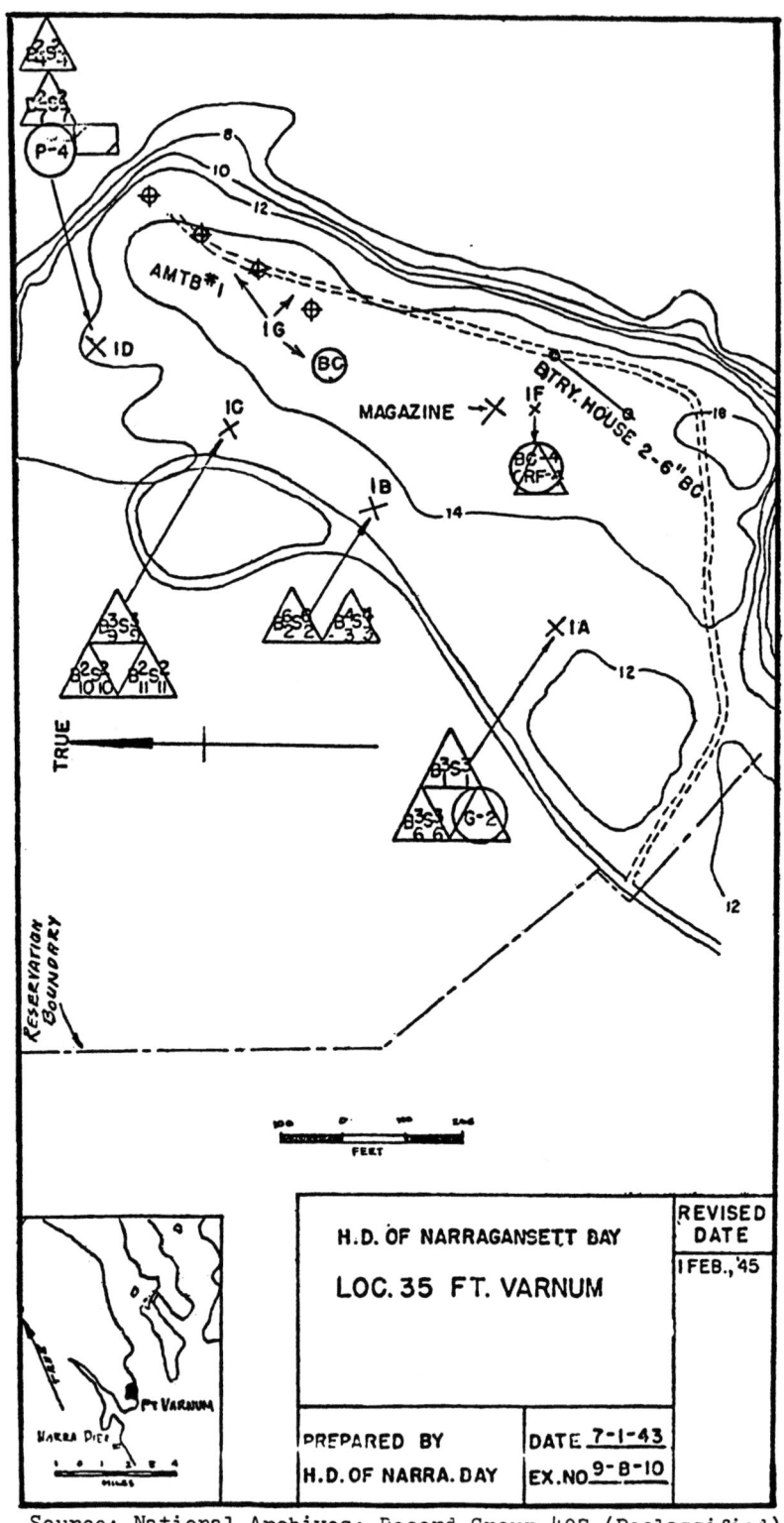

post. The reservation was briefly evacuated on September 14, 1944, because of a hurricane threat. Although extensive property damage resulted from flooding, the Army reoccupied the post the next day.

No. 1 Gun of 6-inch Battery House at Fort Varnum after September 15, 1944 hurricane.

National Archives photo, RG-338.

Fort Varnum, 1979. World War II base end stations do not reveal their age. The former harbor defense site is well maintained by the Rhode Island National Guard.

Photo by author.

The following officers were in command of this fort during World War II:

Capt. James A. Ward	243rd C.A. (HD)	Nov. 28, 1942 - Dec. 1, 1942
Capt. Donald R. Tefft	243rd C.A. (HD)	Dec. 1, 1942 - Jan. 25, 1943
Major Joseph DeRita	243rd C.A. (HD)	Jan. 25, 1943 - Sep. 24, 1943
Lt. Col. Joseph DeRita	243rd C.A. (HD)	Sep. 24, 1943 - Sep. 29, 1943
Major Thomas W. McGrath	243rd C.A. (HD)	Sep. 29, 1943 - Oct. 22, 1943
Capt. William C. Commons, Jr.	243rd C.A. (HD)	Oct. 22, 1943 - Nov. 21, 1943
Major Dean J. Natali	243rd C.A. (HD)	Nov. 21, 1943 - Mar. 12, 1944
Capt. William G. Stagge	243rd C.A. (HD)	Mar. 12, 1944 - Oct. 1, 1944
Capt. William G. Stagge	189th C.A. Bn (HD)	Oct. 1, 1944 - Apr. 6, 1945
Capt. Oskar S. Gulbrandsen	Prov. Bty. Ft. Varnum	Apr. 6, 1945 - Jun. 1, 1946

Minor Installations

When reviewing the military land acquisitions during the World War II era, one focuses readily on the larger reservations discussed earlier and thinks of gun emplacements and troop cantonments simply because they represent what one generally perceives as being typically military. Little attention is paid to the many smaller parcels of land in outlaying and even more distant or isolated areas that were required and utilized for such vital support facilities as fire control and communications stations and sites for radar and searchlight installations. These enclaves were for the most part manned by smaller detachments of specially trained personnel on whom the success or failure of the total defense system depended to no small extent.

A Panama Mount at Brenton Point State Park in Newport.

Photo by author.

Following is a listing of such secondary sites that were directly linked to various designated batteries of the Narragansett Bay Harbor Defense Command, along with information on their uses by Army elements in the early 1940's. Due to repeated mission changes experienced during that period, not all facilities listed were necessarily operational at all times.

Location	Size	Date Acquired	Purpose	Structures
Watch Hill Point	4.6 acres	May 43	Fire Control	Tower, Cottages
Noyes Point	.6 acres	Jan. 42	Fire Control	Tower, Searchlights
Ninigret	.2 acres	May 42	Fire Control	Underground, Searchlight Tower
Charlestown	.9 acres	Apr. 42	Fire Control	Cottages
Green Hill	1.2 acres	May 43	Fire Control	Tower
Green Hill Beach	.4 acres	Nov. 43	Radar	Radar and Searchlight Tower
The Bonnet	.2 acres	Dec. 41	Fire Control (Mine)	Manhole and Searchlights
Hull Cove - Austin Hollow (2 Sites)	1.8 acres	Dec. 42	Fire Control (Mine)	Concrete Casemates - Mine Command 1 & 2
Sachuest Point	18.9 acres	Jan. 42	Fire Control	Cottages, Barn, Silo, Radar, Searchlights
Warren Point (2 sites)	2.7 acres (Total)	Aug. & Oct. 42	Fire Control	Radar, Cottages, Searchlights
Gooseberry Neck	6.5 acres	Mar. 42	Fire Control	Tower, Cottages, Searchlights
Cuttyhunk Island (3 sites)	9 acres (Total)	Jan. 42 - Apr. 43	Fire Control	Concrete Manholes & Searchlights
Gayhead (2 sites)	4 acres (Total)	Feb. 42	Fire Control	Concrete Manholes & Searchlights
Block Island	2 acres	1934	Mil. Res. (Base Camp)	
Block Island (4 sites)	100 acres (Total)	Jun. 42 - Jul. 43	Fire Control	Cottages, Barn, Silo, Radar, Searchlights
Brenton Point (3 sites)	5 acres (Total)	Dec. 41- Dec. 42	Radar & Searchlights	Radar, Searchlights, also Mounts for 155mm Anti Motor Torpedo Boat weapons

Facilities of the types shown above were also located at the sites of various gun batteries in the Bay area.

Searchlight displays were a common sight in the lower Narragansett Bay area during the war.

Photo courtesy A. K. Schroeder, CAMP.

Silent remains at Sachuest Point.

Photo by Author.

Part IV

Army Coast and Harbor Defense Units

EVOLUTION OF COMMAND

Until early December 1941, Rhode Island was a part of the Army's First Coastal Defense District, which embraced the entire coastal area from the Canadian border to the Connecticut-New York State line.

On December 11, 1941, the day Germany declared war on the United States, the First Coastal Defense District was redesignated the New England Frontier Defense Sector, with subsectors established in Portland, Maine; Boston, Massachusetts; and Newport, Rhode Island. The latter included the Harbor Defenses of Narragansett Bay, Long Island Sound and New Bedford, with the Command Post located at Fort Adams.

Additional redesignations took place on January 21, 1942, when the New England Frontier Defense Sector became the New England Sector of the Eastern Theater of Operations, and again on January 9, 1944, when the area was renamed the Northeastern Sector of the Eastern Defense Command. The Sector was disestablished and absorbed into the Eastern Defense Command on May 15, 1945, just days after cessation of hostilities in Europe.

The following senior Army officers commanded the Harbor Defenses of Narragansett Bay from Fort Adams during the periods indicated:

Lt. Col. Randolph T. Pendleton 10th Coast Artillery	Mar. 1940 to Sep. 1940
Colonel Earl C. Webster 243rd Coast Artillery	Sep. 1940 to Mar. 1941
Brig. Gen. Ralph E. Haines	Mar. 1941 to Dec. 1941
Brig Gen. Thomas H. Jones	Dec. 1941
Brig. Gen. Arthur G. Campbell	Dec. 1941 to Oct. 1943
Colonel C. P. Peirce	Oct. 1943 to Feb. 1946

SHIFTING PRIORITIES

With construction of the new and more powerful seacoast batteries at Forts Greene and Church nearing completion, and the forward movement of reinforced units to these sites accomplished, the Army's buildup in the Narragansett Bay area reached its pinnacle in late 1943. During the time the coastal defenses were being strengthened, the threat of an assault on our eastern shores was becoming less likely each day. These circumstances, combined with other more pressing needs, prompted the Army to proceed with a gradual cutback in its harbor defense construction program concurrent with retrenchments in ground forces including those committed to the Narragansett Bay area.

Despite repeated movement of harbor defense units within the Bay area during the war years, the tabulations in the Appendix provide a good insight into the tactical assignments of troops and weapons at specific times.

Headquarters, 243rd Coast Artillery (HD), General Order No. 1 of January 12, 1944, provides a record of weapons fired by this Regiment during the period January 1942 through December 1943. It is interesting to note that the guns of the older pre-World War II batteries at Forts Wetherill, Getty and Kearney were indeed fired, if only for practice. This document also serves to identify various other armaments, stationary and mobile, assigned to elements of the 243rd and locations from where these weapons were fired.

General Order No. 26 and Change 1 issued at Fort Adams by Headquarters Harbor Defenses of Narragansett Bay under dates of December 13 and 31, 1943, provide a complete listing of the assignments made to units of the 10th and 243rd Coast Artillery Regiments.

In General Order No. 5 of February 7, 1944, the Narragansett Bay Harbor Defense Command instituted major changes in the regimental assignments. The responsibility for the mining operation, anti-motor torpedo boat operation, and 6" Battery No. 212 at Fort Church were transferred to the 243rd. Concurrently, the 10th CA Regiment took over the 16" seacoast guns of Battery Hamilton at Fort Greene for a short period of time, manning also the 3" fixed antiaircraft batteries at Forts Wetherill and Adams and moving two of its battery-sized units to Forts Wetherill and Getty without tactical assignments. These transfers were the beginning of that Regiment's pullout. On March 12, 1944, the 10th Coast

Artillery Regiment departed the area for Camp Forrest, Tennessee, and reassignment of its personnel to the 658th, 659th, 790th and 791st Field Artillery Battalions. The Regiment had made Rhode Island, and Fort Adams, its home for 20 years.

[Reproduction of General Order No. 1, Headquarters 243d Coast Artillery (HD), Fort Getty, R.I., 12 January 1944, tabulating scores of target practices conducted by batteries of the regiment from 1 January 1942 to 31 December 1943.]

Anticipating the transfer, Headquarters Harbor Defenses of Narragansett Bay issued General Order No. 7 on February 22, 1944, causing a further reorganization of the 243rd Coast Artillery Regiment. Not only were the 16" batteries no longer manned, but coastal defense needs had diminished to the point that various elements of the Regiment were earmarked as "surplus," available for reassignment. The reorganization was so extensive that most of the units emerged with new unit designations, even though most of their weapons assignments remained unchanged.

General Order No. 8 of February 29, 1944, assigned operation of a seacoast radar and searchlight to each of Batteries 211, 212 and 213. Battery 'G', located at Fort Adams at that time, maintained antiaircraft searchlight installations at Fort Greene and North Point, and dual searchlights at Forts Varnum and Wetherill and at Beavertail, as well as at Brenton and Sachuest Points. Under a subsequent change to General Order No. 8, issued on July 13, 1944, the 37mm weapons of AMTB 1 and 3 were replaced with 40mm guns. At the same time AMTB 3 was pulled back from Brenton Point and assigned to Fort Wetherill.

Having operated with only two battalions since late February, the 243rd Coast Artillery Regiment was disbanded altogether on September 29, 1944, and two newly constituted units, the 188th Coast Artillery Battalion (HD) and 189th Coast Artillery Battalion (HD), resulted from that reorganization. These changes were effected through the redesignation of existing units and the transfer of assigned personnel without major physical relocations.

Lt. Col. Francis N. Spry assumed command of the 188th under General Order No. 1, issued at Fort Wetherill on October 1, 1944. The battallion then had an authorized strength of 31 officers and warrant officers and 570 enlisted personnel.

The 189th was formed at Fort Adams under the command of Lt. Col. Joseph DeRita on October 2, 1944, with a strength of 21 officers and warrant officers and a complement of 391 enlisted men.

As part of the foregoing reorganization, Headquarters, Harbor Defenses of Narragansett Bay, was redesignated Headquarters and Headquarters Battery, Harbor Defenses of Narragansett Bay, with 26 officers and warrant officers and 181 enlisted personnel assigned to this Command.

Additional significant cutbacks took place between March 29 and April 1, 1945, when Headquarters Northeastern Sector, Boston, ordered a further reorganization of the Harbor Defenses of Narragansett Bay.

Batteries not redesignated were inactivated and the personnel reassigned or discharged, while the units retained under the above orders engaged in harbor mine-clearing operations and maintenance of the facilities and 6" batteries at

Forts Greene and Church. When finally deactivated in 1946, these units emerged with still different designations once again identifying them with the Rhode Island National Guard.

PART V.

Within The Bay

NAVAL EXPANSION

The expansion of the naval shore establishment in the Narragansett Bay area during World War II is a story unto itself. The first construction projects to enlarge existing facilities in Newport got under way during the summer of 1940. Simultaneously, ground was broken for a Naval Air Station at Quonset Point. The tempo increased during the spring and summer of 1941. At that time a large portion of the U.S. Atlantic Fleet, including six battleships, eight cruisers, thirty destroyers, two submarines, two destroyer tenders, and two supply ships, was based in the Newport area under the command of Fleet Admiral Ernest J. King. These units were in addition to a group of smaller naval vessels regularly assigned to Narragansett Bay. The supply department of the Naval Training Station was tasked with providing services and supplies to the fleet. To cope with the increased requirements, a series of temporary warehouses was erected at Coddington Cove. By October, railroad spurs had been laid and roads and pier facilities constructed. The supply operation grew to the point that it was designated an independent operation in June 1942, and was named the Naval Supply Depot, Newport. This facility processed tens of thousands of tons of incoming and outgoing stores, provisions and materials around the clock in support of the ships at anchorage and the many thousands of naval personnel undergoing training at the various facilities located in the Bay area. The depot also maintained a Cold Storage Plant in Providence. The capital ships of the fleet were eventually assigned to the war zones; nevertheless, many warships, including heavy and light cruisers, destroyers, escort vessels, and Quonset-based aircraft carriers, made Narragansett Bay a frequent port-of-call or home port throughout the war years.

The naval shore facilities in Rhode Island played a vital role in meeting the needs of the fighting forces during World War II. The significance of these facilities to the war effort becomes evident upon review of the accomplishments of the individual installations.

Naval Training Station

The first on-shore recruit training facility of the Navy was established on Coasters Harbor Island off Newport in 1883. Acquired from the City of Newport in 1881, the 93.5-acre site became known as the Naval Training Station. In 1884, Commodore Stephen B. Luce founded and established the Naval War College at this location, the oldest institution of this type in the world. He became the first President of this prestigious establishment.

In the early days of the Training Station, recruits were housed in tents on shore or on board the USS *New Hampshire*, a double-deck frigate berthed at the island. Later, the USS *Constellation* joined the training ships in the Bay. In 1887, 300 recruits were in training, and by 1901 about 2,000 recruits were being processed through the Training Station each year.

In 1913 the Navy acquired the Government Landing in downtown Newport and constructed a hospital adjacent to the Coasters Harbor Island property on 15 acres of land procured in 1909. During World War I the Navy added 150 acres at Coddington Point on the mainland to its holdings to accommodate a heavy influx of troops into the area at that time. After that war, a period of retrenchment and relative quiet followed.

At the time Germany invaded Poland in 1939, the activities of the Naval Training Station were centered on Coasters Harbor Island, with the Coddington Point area used primarily as a rifle range. In 1940 that site was reactivated and new

Newport Section Base Inshore Patrol, Long Wharf, Newport, October 1943.

Photo courtesy Naval War College archives.

5"/38 Gun Line, Naval Training Station, Newport. Gould Island and Conanicut Island in background.

Photo courtesy Naval War College archives.

berthing, capable of housing 2,770 men, was constructed within 30 days in anticipation of increased recruit intake. Additional land was acquired at Coddington Cove. In 1941 the docks at Long Wharf in Newport were taken over by the newly formed Inshore Patrol. In early 1943 new barracks and facilities to accommodate 9,000 men were constructed in the Coddington Point area.

The Station, dedicated to recruit training in 1939, continued this mission until February 1944. Following Pearl Harbor various service schools were added, and in 1942 a Reserve Officers Indoctrination School was established. In short order it prepared 1,600 officers for active duty assignment. Commencing in December 1943, the Station gradually evolved into a large Ship Pre-Commissioning Center, training crews for specific duties with units of the rapidly expanding fleet.

The Station had a capacity for berthing 2,100 recruits in 1939. This number was exceeded in December of that year when 2,209 trainees were on board. To preclude a potential overflow of personnel, the number of incoming trainees was reduced in early 1940 to 600 per month. By June, the on-board strength had dropped to 1,459. The facilities and berthing expansion program proceeded rapidly, nevertheless, soon providing the Station with the capability of receiving, billeting and training recruits in previously unprecedented numbers over the next few years.

Following is a tabulation of the number of trainees aboard the Naval station at given times:

Year	High	Low
1939	2,093 December	Unknown
1940	3,845 November	1,459 May
1941	6,353 December	1,514 May
1942	16,365 August	5,440 May
1943	12,852 July	7,062 December
1944	2,045 January	0 April

During the above period, a total of 204,115 recruits received training at the Naval Training Station in Newport, Rhode Island.

Commanding Officer's Saturday Inspection on Kidd Field, Coddington Point, Newport.

Photo courtesy Naval War College archives.

Among the smaller facilities constructed in 1942 which actively supported the Navy's training mission in the Newport area were a small arms firing range at Sachuest Point and the Anti Aircraft Training Center at Price's Neck near Brenton Point. The latter installation provided instruction and training in the operation of a wide variety of antiaircraft weapons in the Navy's arsenal, ranging from the smaller .30-caliber machine gun to the larger 40mm and 3" guns. The Center established a fine production record of its own. As an example, a total of 14,000 personnel, including 1,000 officers, received their automatic and heavy weapons training at this facility during the month of November 1943 alone. Many of those passing through this Center were afforded opportunities to practice fire more than one type of weapon.

Anti Aircraft Training Center, Price's Neck, October 1943.
Photo courtesy Naval War College archives.

Naval Torpedo Station

This facility, originally established as an experimental torpedo station on July 29, 1869, was located on Goat Island in the East Passage off Newport. The long history of this 32-acre site is closely associated with the early defenses of Newport Harbor. As far back as 1700, the British had caused the construction of a small earthen battery on the island, which was found inadequate for the defense of the harbor. In 1702 a larger fortification was ordered built, and when completed was named Fort Anne in honor of the Queen of England. In 1730 the name was changed to Fort George. On December 5, 1774, the Assembly of Rhode Island ordered the fort dismantled.

When Rhode Island declared her independence on May 4, 1776, the fort was reconstructed under the name of Fort Liberty. It later fell into the hands of the British, who used the fort's twenty-five 18- and 24-pound cannon against the French during the campaign for Rhode Island on July 29, 1778. In 1784 the site was given the name Fort Washington, and in 1798 it was rechristened Fort Wolcott to commemorate the Revolutionary War services of Governor Abner Wolcott.

The Town of Newport turned Goat Island over to the Federal Government in 1799. The Army controlled the property until 1869, when Commander E. O. Matthews, USN, assumed command of the newly established Naval Torpedo

View of Goat Island in May 1909. Remains of Fort Wolcott earthworks in right foreground.

U. S. Naval Historical Center photo.

Station. From the very beginning the facility actively engaged in developing torpedoes and other forms of naval ordnance. A gun-cotton storage facility was activated nearby in 1883 in support of the station and was designated U.S. Naval Magazine, Rose Island.

During World War I the station employed some 3,200 civilian workers when it developed and produced depth charges, mines, and torpedoes for the fleet. Of special note is the increased production of primers achieved in 1918 as a direct result of employing women munitions workers, who have been credited with outproducing their male counterparts by six to one.

Torpedo Station, Goat Island, Newport.
Photo courtesy Naval Facilities Engineering Command archives.

At that time the Navy established a storage facility for high explosives on Gould Island off Conanicut Island in the East Passage. This 56-acre tract was placed under the jurisdiction of the Goat Island facility. Over the next few years several buildings were erected on Gould Island for torpedo and warhead storage and for housing a detachment of Marines. In 1921, two seaplanes were assigned to the torpedo station to experiment with airdropped torpedoes. For this purpose hangars were constructed at the southern end of Gould Island and ramps were installed for accessibility of the planes to and from the waters of Narragansett Bay. Despite the continuing role of the station in developing and perfecting the Navy's weapons arsenal after World War I, the workforce had been reduced to 927 personnel by 1923.

As part of a general assessment of naval installations in the Newport area, the station was inspected by President Franklin D. Roosevelt, Secretary of the Navy Frank Knox, Senator Theodore F. Green of Rhode Island, and other dignitaries on August 12, 1940. By the end of that year, the employment figures of the station had swelled to 4,802 workers, up approximately 1,000 in twelve months. Following the state of emergency declared by the President on May 27, 1941, the station went through a period of rapid expansion. Additional torpedo storage facilities were leased on Third Street and at Long Wharf in Newport, and in Fall River. At that time the station also assumed work in support of British torpedo ranging and overhaul requirements. In February 1942, Gould Island was provided the capability to proof fire 100 torpedoes per day, while personnel of the MTB Squadrons Training Station in Melville were preparing to set up a PT boat torpedo overhaul facility in the shops on Goat Island. The Marine Barracks at the Torpedo Station was disbanded and moved to Coddington Cove in October 1942, where a torpedo station annex consisting of ten concrete and

President Roosevelt on inspection tour of Naval installations in the Newport area, August 12, 1940. With the President: Navy Secretary Frank Knox, Senator T. F. Green of Rhode Island, Admiral Kalbfus, and Captain Welch.

Photo courtesy National Archives, FDR Library.

earth-covered torpedo storage magazines was also established. Additional buildings were constructed to house various offices and functions that were being relocated from the main production facility on Goat Island. In early 1944, a 'K'-type blimp from South Weymouth was assigned to assist in observing the proof firing of torpedoes.

Gould Island, August 18, 1943. Seaplane hangar in foreground; torpedo testing facility in the distance.

U. S. Naval Historical Center photo.

A Naval Magazine established on Prudence Island in April 1942 was placed under the control of the Torpedo Station on July 8, 1944. By August of that year, the Torpedo Station had become the largest single industrial-type employer in the State of Rhode Island, with more than 12,600 employees, including many women, on its payroll. The facility operated 24 hours a day, seven days a week.

Later in the year a degaussing station, i.e., a demagnetizing facility capable of neutralizing ships to prevent their attracting or detonating magnetic mines or torpedoes, was put into operation on Gould Island.

Rose Island, October 31, 1943. Antiaircraft batteries emplaced near lighthouse.

U. S. Naval Historical Center photo.

Abandoned WW II ammunition storage facilities on Prudence Island.

NOAA photo 10-14-53-J-2186.

The Naval Torpedo Station held a position of vital importance to the war effort, having produced approximately one third of the 57,653 torpedoes manufactured for the U.S. Navy during the period January 1, 1939, to June 1, 1946.

Naval Operating Base

The establishment of the Naval Operating Base in Newport was promulgated under Navy Department Orders No. 145 on March 31, 1941. This action had the effect of grouping the various naval shore activities then in being under a single headquarters for the purpose of coordinating common functions and activities and of providing services to the operating elements. Six hundred two-story housing units, each with four dwellings, were built and placed under the administration of the Naval Operating Base in August 1941.

Naval Fuel Depot

In step with the development of steam-powered ships, the Navy in 1900 established a fleet coaling station at Melville, one of the largest of its kind in the country. Situated in Portsmouth on the east shore of Narragansett Bay, the 160-acre facility in its early day attracted many battleships and cruisers to anchorages in the East Passage to take on coal. By 1917 the station had evolved into a general fuel depot, with on-shore fuel oil storage capacity reaching in excess of 13 million gallons by 1937. This depot continued to play a vital fleet support role during World War II, when substantial additional storage capacity, including two off-site tank farms, were added to the existing facilities.

Naval Net Depot

The Secretary of the Navy ordered the establishment of a torpedo and submarine net facility at the fuel depot in Melville effective February 15, 1941. Lt. Leonard W. Bailey, USN, became the first officer to command this new operation. He also took charge of the fuel depot.

A school was soon organized to train naval officers and enlisted men in the art of harbor net defenses. As Narragansett Bay held a high priority among naval fleet anchorages, the design and production of netting required to meet local needs was initiated without delay. For this purpose a concrete slab 200' x 300' was constructed, the first of its kind in the United States. The heavy steel nets were woven around pins inserted into the slab.

Following the attack on Pearl Harbor in December 1941, the Melville Group was tasked with producing netting capable of preventing passage of small two-man submarines, a type in the Japanese arsenal. Depot personnel, in designing the layout of the net slab, had taken factors of this sort into account and were able to respond quickly to the Navy's critical needs. Melville at that time was the only facility in existence with the capability of producing the required configuration of submarine nets.

New warehouses were constructed and quickly filled with buoys, baulks, torpedo netting, chain and anchors, which arrived via rail by the carload.

Concrete slab at antitorpedo net production facility in Melville, July 1941.

Photo Naval War College archives.

The first contingent of trainees arrived on April 1, 1941, when billeting spaces were still scarce. This necessitated housing the officers in town and assigning the enlisted men to barracks at the Naval Training Station several miles away. Buses daily carried the men to their duty stations. Due to the initial lack of facilities at the depot, the first group of officers commenced their training at the Armory on Thames Street in Newport. After approximately one month, the training site was relocated in Melville. Groups of 15 officers and 30 men were graduated from the net school every three months during 1941. While some of the men put their newly acquired skills to work in setting up the net defenses of Narragansett Bay, others shipped out to perform similar duties at other locations. Personnel of the net depot also eventually operated the gate tenders USS *YNG-2* and USS *YNG-11* in the East Passage.

On orders of the Chief of Naval Operations, the unit formed a Net and Boom Defense Experimental Group in 1942 when it became apparent that improvements in existing net defenses were necessary.

Motor Torpedo Boat Squadrons Training Center

In December 1941, the Navy had three squadrons of PT boats (Patrol Torpedo Boats) at its disposal. Two of these were stationed in the Pacific area while a third unit was being outfitted at the New York Naval Shipyard prior to deployment to the Canal Zone.

Although untried under combat conditions until this time, the PTs in the Pacific area of operations soon met the test of action under fire and proved their worth during the first difficult months of the war.

Following the commissioning of Squadron 4 on January 13, 1942, and designation of this unit as the training squadron, the Secretary of the Navy on February 17, 1942, directed the establishment of the MTB Squadrons Training Center at Melville, Rhode Island. LCDR William C. Specht, USN, was placed in command of the Center with the responsibility of carrying out the vital training mission which would allow for expansion of needed MTB capabilities.

Quonset huts at the U.S. Naval Motor Torpedo Squadrons Training Center, January 1944.

Courtesy Naval Facilities Engineering Command archives.

The first group of 51 officers and 177 enlisted personnel was actively engaged in training by the first week of April. Forty-seven Quonset huts were erected in short order to meet the immediate needs of the new Center. Ultimately the facilities were expanded to provide housing for up to 90 student officers and 860 enlisted trainees. In due course the MTB Training Center comprised 197 Quonset huts designated as living quarters, 13 offices, 34 classrooms and 42 maintenance buildings. A total of 28 PT boats of 4 distinct types was assigned to the squadron by the end of 1944.

The original two-month training period was extended to three months in 1943 for officers and certain specialty enlisted rates. Extensive use of the facilities at the Naval Anti Aircraft Training Center at Price's Neck, the Naval Torpedo Station, and the Naval Training Center's rifle range was made by the PT boaters. Trainees were also detailed to factory training at the Packard Engine School in Detroit and the Elco plant, manufacturer of PT boats, at Bayonne, New Jersey.

By mid-August 1945, when the Navy had a total of 30 operational PT boat squadrons, the Melville Training Center had trained 2,017 officers and 17,500 enlisted men. All of the active units with the exception of Squadron 4 were decommissioned by the end of 1945, while two new squadrons were organized. These units were also decommissioned by mid-April 1946.

While in the Narragansett Bay area, the PT boats of Squadron 4 actively engaged in patrolling operations off the Rhode Island coast and acted as listening posts farther out at sea.

PT boats in formation were a common sight in Narragansett Bay during the war years.

Courtesy Office of Naval History.

Naval Air Station

During the 1938-39 period the Navy was seeking suitable locations for the establishment of new naval air bases. A board designated to study various alternatives recommended the Quonset Point area in Rhode Island as one of two East Coast locations selected. In May 1939, President Roosevelt approved a bill providing $1,000,000 for the acquisition of the land and, on June 26, 1940, an appropriation in excess of $24 million for construction of the new naval facility.

The area selected comprised 750 acres on the West Passage at the southern end of Quidnesset in the Town of North Kingstown. Until then, the property had been utilized as farmland and a summer colony. A smaller adjacent area had been acquired by the State of Rhode Island in 1892 and used by the Militia. During the Spanish-American War that parcel became the site of a Recruiting and Training Station. In World War I it was again used for training purposes. The State Guard and subsequently the Rhode Island National Guard had held their summer field encampments in this rural area. When the Navy acquired the Quonset area in 1939, the State offered the campsite and a small airstrip on the property to the Government.

Construction of what was to become the largest naval air facility in the East got under way in July 1940. Estimated to result in a two- or three-year construction project, the work planned originally was completed in July 1941; however, work added to the original scope of the project extended the total construction effort into 1943. A total of 11,000 civilian workers, men and women of all trades and professions, were engaged around the clock, seven days a week, to complete what was described as "the biggest and toughest, yet most rapidly progressing construction project ever undertaken on the Atlantic coast." Many of the workers were from Rhode Island.

Actual work extended beyond the mainland to Hope Island and into the Bay. To provide a deep-water channel for ships, 19 million cubic yards of sand and mud were dredged from Narragansett Bay and deposited along the perimeter of the construction site, thus providing the Navy with an additional 270 acres of usable area, which it utilized for the installation of required runways. Overall area gained through landfill totalled approximately 400 acres. To further emphasize the magnitude of the project, one need only consider that in addition to the construction of four landplane and two seaplane hangars, control towers, barracks for 1,680 men and other vital troop and operational facililties, 100 tons of asphalt were being laid down each hour; underground storage for three million gallons of gasoline was being provided, and an aircraft carrier pier 80' wide and 1,172' long was under construction. Housing capacity for 15,000 men was ultimately provided.

Loading operations at Quonset Pier, July 3, 1941.
Photo courtesy Naval Facilities Engineering Command archives.

On October 10, 1940, a scouting squadron was commissioned at Quonset to support the Navy's Neutrality Patrol. Until then, several seaplanes operating from the hangars on Gould Island had been assigned this mission.

The Naval Air Station was officially commissioned on July 12, 1941, under the command of Commander Andrew C. Fall, USN. The ceremonies were attended by Rear Admiral Edward C. Kalbfus, then Commandant of the Newport Naval Station. An Assembly and Repair Department was put into operation on August 21 of that year. Among other early activities at the new facility was the establishment of a Naval Training School for the indoctrination of Reserve Officers. Large groups of graduates were turned out every three months. The term "90-day wonders" may well have found its origin here. Later, as training facilities at the Training Station in Newport became overcrowded, a boot camp for basic trainees was established at Quonset.

British pilots were sent to NAS Quonset Point to receive training in the operation of U.S. fighter aircraft which were being supplied to Great Britain. In due course several British squadrons were assigned to the station. The first "Seabees" were also trained at Quonset while the base for the Construction Battalions was still being built.

In October 1944, NAS Quonset Point became the seat of the Commander, Naval Air Bases, First Naval District. This action placed four Naval Air Stations, a Coast Guard Station, 17 Naval Auxiliary Air Facilities and five smaller air facilities scattered between Groton, Connecticut, and Bar Harbor, Maine, under the Quonset Command.

Several of the auxiliary fields were located in the State of Rhode Island. The Naval Auxiliary Air Facility in Charlestown, built in 1942 with berthing for 696 personnel, became well known for its night-fighter operations. Redesignated as an Auxiliary Landing Facility, the field was later primarily used by Quonset-based fliers for carrier landing practice. The other activities were known as the Naval Auxiliary Air Facility in Westerly and the Air Detail, Gould Island.

Quonset-based aircraft carriers and planes participated actively in antisubmarine warfare, convoy escort duties, and air and sea rescue missions, as well as in air patrol operations in coastal areas.

The Davisville Complex

Located on the Quidnessett peninsula North of Quonset, this complex stretched from the Bay westward four miles to Post Road and included a smaller triangular area adjacent to the main railway line west of that road. It received its name "Davisville" from the nearest railroad station, located at the westernmost perimeter of the installation.

Authority to organize the first Naval Construction Company since World War I was granted on October 31, 1941. By December, ninety-nine enlisted men and two Civil Engineer Corps officers were in training at the Naval Training Station in Newport, Rhode Island. That same month establishment of four more companies was authorized. These units were to become the builder-fighters of the Navy, constructing facilities under fire while defending themselves and their works in the face of the enemy.

On February 27, 1942, the Davisville Advance Base Depot, the first of its kind, and an outgrowth of an 85-acre temporary facility activated in March 1941, was established.

Tasked with purchasing, storing and processing materials and equipment that would be required for the construction of advance bases overseas, the new facility was expanded to cover a total of 1,892 acres adjacent to Quonset Point. A pier 1,200' x 250' was constructed, 56 buildings erected, rail spurs laid and in excess of 13 million square feet of open storage area graded or paved. Shipments of advance base material from this depot amounted to 226,000 long tons in 1942; 336,000 in 1943; 498,000 in 1944; and 253,000 through the first eight months of 1945.

Dedication of Camp Endicott, Naval Construction Training Center, Davisville.

Photo Naval Facilities Engineering Command archives.

To meet the Navy's accelerating needs for larger numbers of Seabees (short for Construction Battalions), a Naval Construction Training Center was established at Davisville under the name of "Camp Endicott" and dedicated on June 27, 1942. This camp was given its name in honor of Rear Admiral Mordecai T. Endicott, first Civil Engineer Corps officer of the Navy to become Chief of the Bureau of Yards and Docks.

Here, as in the case of the sister facility at Quonset Point, contractor personnel had but a minimum amount of time to meet the construction deadlines of the rapidly expanding naval shore establishment. Facilities to house, train and support 25 officers and 1,071 enlisted men were completed in a short 59 days; the first units commenced basic and advanced training on August 12, 1942.

The Navy's builder-fighters with the 'CAN DO' motto.
Photo Naval Facilities Engineering Command archives.

The Center reached its full capacity of 350 officers and 15,000 men in November of that year. That made it necessary to establish an administrative unit responsible for receiving incoming troops (who were by then arriving in ever-increasing numbers), maintaining permanent station forces, and processing the transients upon completion of training. This was accomplished by separating a small area from the Advance Base Depot. The new area created was designated "Camp Thomas" in honor of Captain Robert E. Thomas, Civil Engineer Corps, United States Navy, who had perished in a plane crash. The operations of the Depot continued uninterrupted, receiving and shipping approximately one-half million tons of cargo each year.

The Civil Engineer Officers Training School — originally located on the 11,000-acre reservation of Camp Peary near Williamsburg, Virginia — was moved to Camp Endicott, Rhode Island, effective May 11, 1944. The initial curriculum included a four-week Indoctrination Course for officers commissioned from civilian life or from enlisted status, and several four-week offerings in Basic and Advanced Construction Battalion and Public Works operations. The Frenchtown Naval Reservation on Route 2 in East Greenwich, then called Sun Valley, was used extensively by the school. It was at this 6,800-acre site that the officers demonstrated their knowledge and skills under field conditions.

Various specialty courses were added to the officers' training program during the summer of 1944. Among these were a Port Director School, to familiarize participants with cargo stowing and discharge operations, and a Pontoon Officer's Course, as well as courses in Sanitary Engineering, Public Works and Advance Base Familiarization. The School also arranged for sessions with representatives from private industry to familiarize the private sector with Construction Battalion operations and requirements. In May 1945 the training school was fully integrated into the organization of the Naval Construction Training Center.

The average number of naval civil engineering officers undergoing training at Davisville at any one time was approximately 600, ranging from a low of 260 to a high of 900. Over a 15-month period 9,000 naval officers were prepared here for Construction Battalion and Public Works duties.

By the end of the war a total of 100,000 men had received their training at Davisville. This equated to 90 Mobile Construction Battalions and 25 Seabee Base Maintenance Units that had been trained, equipped and put into the field. Many of these men received additional specialized training at Quonset Point prior to being shipped overseas.

In 1943 an Advance Base Proving Ground was also put into operation within the Davisville Complex. It was responsible for researching and developing hundreds of pieces of equipment which the Naval Construction Forces would be required to operate and handle in remote areas overseas. Experimentation with pontoons was one of several items that received special emphasis. Used as drydocks, bridges, ferries, and barges, the Davisville-developed pontoons deployed around the world were of critical importance to the invasions of Sicily, North Africa and Normandy, locations where they were assembled to form causeways to facilitate the movement of advancing troops, equipment and supplies.

Storage and production facilities at Davisville during World War II.
Photo Naval Facilities Engineering Command archives.

Typical of the ingenuity, spirit and responsiveness of the private sector to the demands of the time were the development and quantity production of compact, portable shelters required by the Navy in meeting its responsibilities of establishing advance bases overseas and, in particular, in supporting the expansion of military facilities in Great Britain under the Lend Lease Act of March 1941. In less than one month after the Navy made its needs known to representatives of the George A. Fuller Company and of the Merritt, Chapman and Scott Corporation, both primary contractors in the construction of the Naval Air Station, plans were presented for the manufacture of an inexpensive, compact and lightweight structure of corrugated steel that was highly portable and also easily erected. A prompt 'go ahead' was given the G. A. Fuller Company and a factory was built at West Davisville in record time. Within three months after the problem had been presented, the Navy shipped the first shelters from its new pier facilities at the rapidly developing Air Station. The shelters were known as "Quonset huts." A second factory was

A row of Quonset huts on deserted No Mans Land Island.
Photo courtesy R. I. Port Authority.

built and soon 3,000 workers were producing $22 million worth of Quonset huts per year. These local facilities manufactured 32,253 units during the war, while many more were produced in plants that sprang up across the country in response to total military demands. By the end of the war, the Navy alone had erected in excess of 150,000 of these unique structures. Quonset huts, which gave the appearance of a semicircular arch in cross-section, were a modified version of the older British World War I-type Nisson hut. Because the basic structure was so simple in design and readily adaptable to a wide variety of field uses, it soon found its way to the most distant and isolated allied posts around the globe.

ANTIAIRCRAFT DEFENSES

While the permanent 3" antiaircraft gun installations at Forts Adams and Wetherill and certain smaller caliber automatic weapons deployed further south were tasked with protecting the harbor defense sites against aerial attack and the minefields from shipboard interference, the Navy initially provided most of the weapons required for the antiaircraft defenses of its own vital installations, i.e., the Torpedo Station and the Naval Air Station at Quonset Point.

Within one month after the United States entered the war in December 1941, the Navy commenced the installation of 20mm guns at the Torpedo Station on Goat Island. Gun crews were assigned to these weapons at the beginning of March 1942. Additional emplacements for antiaircraft guns of various sizes were concurrently being readied at a number of other locations in the Newport area.

During the first days of April, the 207th Coast Artillery Regiment, a semi-mobile New York National Guard antiaircraft unit then on duty at Camp Pendleton, Virginia, bagan moving into Newport. Colonel Ralph C. Tobin, Commanding Officer, deployed the first elements of the Regiment to Goat and Gould Islands, where they relieved the Navy gun crews on April 5, 1942. The balance of the Regiment arrived during the next two months, initially finding shelter at the Naval Operating Base until assigned to permanent battery locations in the Newport area.

Coasters Harbor Island, July 1942. Antiaircraft gun emplacements adjacent to the Naval War College.

Navy photo.

Army sentry at gate to antiaircraft gun installations on Coasters Harbor Island. Sims Hall in rear.

Navy photo.

On May 8, 1942, Lieutenant General Hugh A. Drum, USA, accompanied by Major General Sanford Jarman and Brigadier General Olin H. Longino of the 36th Coast Artillery Brigade, inspected the Army antiaircraft units assigned to the Newport naval installations. During this visit the Commanding General paid a courtesy call on Admiral Royal Ingersoll, Commander-in-Chief, Atlantic Fleet, aboard the USS *Constellation*, then tied up at Coasters Harbor Island, site of the Naval Training Station.

The 207th Coast Artillery (AA) remained in the area until relieved by the 701st Coast Artillery Regiment (Anti Aircraft) a year later in April 1943. At that time the personnel of the 701st were assigned to the following locations and weapons:

Navy equipment operated by Army personnel:		
Naval Training Station	Three (3)	5" 25 Caliber Antiaircraft Guns
Goat Island	Three (3)	1.1" Quadruple Mounts
	Twelve (12)	20mm Machine Guns
Gould Island	Four (4)	1.1" Quadruple Mounts
Naval Air Station, Quonset	Twenty-four (24)	20mm Machine Guns

Army installed and operated equipment:		
Rose Island	Four (4)	90mm Antiaircraft Guns
	Two (2)	50 Caliber Machine Guns
Ruggles Avenue, Newport	Four (4)	90mm Antiaircraft Guns
	Two (2)	50 Caliber Machine Guns
Naval Training Station	Two (2)	50 Caliber Machine Guns
Eustis Avenue, Newport	Four (4)	90mm Antiaircraft Guns
	Three (3)	50 Caliber Machine Guns
Naval Air Station, Quonset	Eight (8)	40mm Antiaircraft Guns

The 90mm guns at the above locations replaced Navy 5" 25 caliber antiaircraft guns which had been removed in mid-April 1943. The Army units also installed and operated 18 searchlights in support of their antiaircraft defense mission.

Ruggles Avenue, Newport, in July 1942. Antiaircraft gun installation under construction.

Navy photo.

One month after the successful June 6, 1944, Normandy Beach landing in Europe, the 701st was pulled out of Newport and transferred to Fort Dix, New Jersey. Dismantling of the Navy's antiaircraft guns commenced shortly thereafter.

While assigned to the Bay area, units of both the 207th and the 701st CA (AA) Regiments were relieved from time to time by the Automatic Weapons Battalion of the 540th Anti Aircraft Artillery to allow the former to participate in maneuvers.

Antiaircraft positions at Eustis Avenue, Newport, July 1943. Gate to military compound was at Loyola Terrace.

Photo Naval War College archives.

Silent remains of the Army's presence in Newport during WW II.

Photos by author.

PART VI

Enemy Nearby

THE DARK DAYS

It was not long after declaring war on the United States that the presence of German submarines was felt by marine interests all along the eastern sea frontier. In announcing a "blockade" of the Atlantic Coast and Caribbean in early 1942, Germany cleared the way for its undersea raiders to attack ships of all flags. The U-boats generally took up positions where their unsuspecting prey could be expected to be most plentiful, and little selectivity was exercised regarding the size of vessel attacked. This is evident by the number of smaller craft that fell victim to the torpedoes or to the deck guns of submarines that surfaced boldly in broad daylight. The prowlers were spotted everywhere along vital shipping lanes and near fishing grounds. The U-boat onslaught along the American coast took on disastrous proportions, particularly during 1942. However, by mid-1943 sophisticated defensive weapons and tactics had been developed that reduced the submarine menace substantially, almost to the level of being no more than a nuisance. This condition continued until the Germans developed snorkel-equipped boats that could remain submerged for weeks. It was not until the waning months of the war, however, that this type of submarine appeared in any appreciable numbers in the Western Atlantic. Although the odds were still against them, these raiders took many chances, more frequently than not resulting in their own demise, to harass U.S. coastal shipping right through the very last days of the war.

Enemy submarines operating off New England sank a total of 12 merchant ships during the period January 14, 1942 to May 5, 1945, resulting in the loss of 205 lives. There were 445 survivors rescued. Following is a listing of the ships lost:

SS NORNESS — 14,000-ton Panamanian tanker: Struck by three torpedoes less than 50 miles south of Martha's Vineyard, Massachusetts, on January 14, 1942. Two crew members lost and 41 survivors brought to Newport, Rhode Island.

SS SKOTTLAND — 2,117-ton Norwegian freighter: Struck by two torpedoes about 65 miles southeast of Mt. Desert Rock, Maine, on May 17, 1942. Ship sank in three minutes with a full load of lumber. One crew member killed. Twenty-three survivors picked up by a lobster boat and taken to Boston.

SS MATTAWIN — 6,130-ton British freighter: Torpedoed approximately 180 miles southeast of Cape Cod, Massachusetts, on June 1, 1942. Eighteen crew members lost. Of 52 survivors rescued, 20 were landed at Nauset, Massachusetts, and 32 at Halifax, Nova Scotia.

BEN & JOSEPHINE — 102-ton American fishing dragger: Sunk on June 3, 1942, through gunfire from surfaced German submarine about 170 miles east of Thatcher's Island, Massachusetts. All six crew members were rescued and brought to Mt. Desert Rock, Maine.

AEOLUS — 41-ton American fishing dragger: Sunk about 170 miles east of Thatcher's Island, Massachusetts, on June 3, 1942, by gunfire from surfaced submarine. All six crew members rescued and landed at Mt. Desert Rock, Maine.

SS CHEROKEE — 5,896-ton American passenger vessel: Struck by two torpedoes on June 5, 1942, about 62 miles east of Provincetown, Massachusetts. Eighty-six of her crew of 169 were lost. Forty-two survivors were landed in Provincetown and 41 in Boston. Enroute from England to New York, the vessel was carrying 42 U.S. Army officers to stateside training assignments and four Russian naval officers. The latter went down with the ship to permit others to escape.

SS PORT NICHOLSON — 8,000-ton British freighter: Took two torpedoes 60 miles east of Provincetown, Massachusetts, on June 15, 1942. All hands abandoned ship. When the vessel remained afloat for eight and one-half hours, the master and first mate reboarded the ship but were lost when it went down. Eighty-three survivors were landed at Boston.

SS ALEXANDER MACOMB — 7,192-ton American freighter: Sunk by a torpedo about 150 miles east of Cape Cod on July 3, 1942. Ten men lost; 56 survivors taken to Woods Hole, Massachusetts, and Halifax, Nova Scotia, by rescue vessels.

EBB — 259-ton American fishing trawler: Enroute from Western to Brown Bank on July 28, 1942, with a catch of 80,000 pounds of fish, this vessel was attacked and sunk by gunfire from a surfaced submarine which continued firing while the crew was abandoning ship. Five men were killed and seven of the twelve survivors wounded.

SS PAN PENNSYLVANIA — 11,017-ton American tanker: Carrying 140,000 barrels of high-octane gasoline and seven planes from New York to England, this ship was struck by torpedo on April 16, 1944, about 75 miles southeast of Nantucket Island, Massachusetts. Twenty-five of her crew of 81 were lost. Depth charges forced the attacking submarine, the U-550, to surface. It was later rammed by destroyer-escort *Gandy* and engaged in a gun duel. The U-550 sank following an on-board explosion. Twelve members of the submarine's crew were rescued. The captains of the *Pan Pennsylvania* and the U-550 were both rescued by the same US warship.

SS CORNWALLIS — 5,458-ton Canadian cargo freighter: Hit by torpedo near Mt. Desert Rock, Maine, on December 3, 1944. The crew was sleeping below deck at the time of the attack. Of 49 men aboard, only five were rescued. The survivors were landed in Rockland, Maine.

SS BLACK POINT — 5,353-ton American collier: Sunk by torpedo about three miles off Point Judith, Rhode Island, on May 5, 1945. Twelve men killed. Her 34 survivors were taken to Point Judith, Newport and Quonset Point. The *Black Point* was the last merchant vessel lost in the Atlantic during World War II.

In addition to the foregoing, the USS *Atlantic States*, an empty 8,537-ton American tanker, was torpedoed nine miles north of Cape Cod Light, Massachusetts, on April 5, 1945. When the boiler room flooded, 52 crew members abandoned ship, were rescued, and were taken to Boston. The captain and four others kept the vessel afloat until it was towed to Boston for repairs. A task group of two frigates and two destroyer escorts under Commander Ralph R. Curry, USCG, located the attacking submarine (U-857) off the tip of Cape Cod, where destroyer escort *Gustafson* destroyed the enemy on April 7 through repeated hedgehog attacks.

U-boats did not confine their activities exclusively to stalking ships. During the latter part of July 1943, the U-230 entered Chesapeake Bay and laid mines off Norfolk.

On November 28, 1944, soon after air and surface patrols were curtailed in the Bar Harbor area, the U-1230 quickly seized the opportunity by landing two agents at Hancock Point.

Earlier actions of this type had taken place on June 13, 1942, when the U-202 landed four saboteurs on a deserted beach near Amagansett, Long Island, and on June 17, 1942, when the U-584 dropped four agents at Ponte Vedra beach in Florida. The threat from these groups was shortlived, however.

A TIME OF RECKONING

In early 1945, the war in Europe was rapidly coming to an end. On April 26, the U.S. First Army, advancing through the heart of Germany, linked up with Russian forces at the town of Torgau on the Elbe River. On May 2, Berlin fell to the Soviets while the British made their first contact with Russian troops in Northern Germany. By May 4, the U.S. Seventh Army, pushing south through Germany, met the advance elements of the U.S. Fifth Army on its northward thrust through Italy.

During the period February to April, the Germans dispatched a number of snorkel-equipped U-boats to the East Coast of the United States in a last desperate attempt to harass Atlantic coastal shipping. However, U.S. anti-submarine forces were so well organized by then that all but three of the undersea prowlers were detected and destroyed before they could reach their assigned operational areas.

U-857 eluded the submarine hunters and moved into the Gulf of Maine in late March, making its presence known on April 5 when it unsuccessfully torpedoed the empty American tanker *Atlantic States* off Highland Light on Cape Cod. The submarine was detected and destroyed on April 7.

The 740-ton snorkeler U-548 scored its first hit on April 14 when it sank the unescorted freighter *Belgian Airman* off Cape Henry. An antisubmarine force consisting of six destroyer escorts from Hampton Roads and a mixed group of destroyers, frigates and gunboats called in from Narragansett Bay, supported by naval aircraft from Norfolk and Elizabeth City and several blimps, launched an intensive hunt for the elusive submarine. On April 18, the U-548 struck again, this time sinking the unescorted tanker *Swiftscout* off the Delaware Capes. Once more the submarine avoided detection, and on April 23 torpedoed the Norwegian tanker *Katy* about 75 miles southeast of Cape Henry; her crew saved the vessel, however. A freighter sighted the U-boat four days later, but it was not until the night of April 29 that the submarine was detected by naval ships just as it was preparing to attack the frigate *Natchez*. The fate of the U-548 was sealed several hours later through effective naval action.

The third undersea raider to reach the U.S. coastal area without being spotted was the 740-ton snorkel-equipped U-853. Commissioned in June 1943, this submarine had seen action in the North Atlantic on May 25, 1944, when it survived an attack by British aircraft while on a weather reporting mission, and again on June 17, when strafed by two fighter planes from the U.S. Carrier *Croatan* after being hunted for several days. In both instances, the U-boat fought back with its deck-mounted antiaircraft guns. During the last engagement, two members of the gun crew were killed and eleven others wounded. Though severely wounded himself, the boat's skipper, Kapitänleutnant Helmut Sommer, managed to take his craft down in time to avoid being bombed by approaching aircraft. Dubbed "Moby Dick" by the crew of the *Croatan* because of her elusiveness, the U-853 vanished once again, arriving in Lorient, France, on July 3, 1944.

Oberleutnant Helmut Frömsdorf, the boat's 24-year old former First Officer, was in command of the submarine when it set out from Norway on February 24, 1945, for operations off the coast of Maine after being rebuilt and outfitted with a snorkel.

On April 23, the USS PE-56, a 340-ton Navy patrol boat used for target-towing assignments, exploded and sank three miles off Cape Elizabeth, Maine, with the loss of 49 officers and men. Although the sinking was officially attributed to a boiler explosion, the 13 survivors believed the PE-56 had been struck by a torpedo or mine. Post-war German researchers have credited the U-853 with the destruction of this patrol vessel.

On the evening of May 4, 1945, Germany's Grand Admiral Doenitz ordered all German warships at sea to cease hostilities and return to port. Whether the U-853 ever received the order is not known. On the afternoon of May 5, she was lurking in Rhode Island coastal waters at periscope depth.

Commissioning of the U-853 in Germany on June 25, 1943.
Photo courtesy Bibliothek für Zeitgeschichte, Germany.

Over the years the Coast Artillery units deployed along the shore of Rhode Island were placed on alert many times as a result of reports by fishermen, merchantmen or Navy and Coast Guard vessels that a submarine had been sighted. On May 5, the 6" guns of Battery 211, emplaced near the Point Judith lighthouse, were once again loaded and ready. As usual, all was calm and quiet. The battery command post, located in one of the camouflaged concrete cottages at the South Reservation of Fort Greene, was operational. On this sunny afternoon, Block Island was clearly visible 11 miles away on the horizon. About four miles south of Point Judith the 5,353-ton collier *Black Point* was leisurely making its way from New York to Boston with a load of soft coal, travelling in the safety of the coastal waterway between Long Island Sound and the Cape Cod Canal.

At about 5:40 p.m., just as the *Black Point* was entering the western end of Rhode Island Sound four miles southeast of Point Judith, an explosion pierced the silence, tearing away 40 feet of the ship's after section. The ship settled rapidly by the stern, rolled to port and sank in less than 25 minutes. While Army gunners were scurrying about on shore, frantically trying to spot the marauding submarine, several vessels were converging on the scene to assist in rescue operations. Thirty-four survivors, including three injured, were picked up by the Yugoslav freighter *Kamen* and the Coast Guard 83-footers *Hornbeam* and *Hibiscus*. A total of twelve men were lost, several when the torpedo struck and exploded.

Within minutes of the attack, SS *Kamen* sent out an SOS, reporting the location of the ill-fated collier. Coast Guard frigate *Moberly* (PF-63), travelling in the company of Navy destroyer escorts *Amick* (DE-168) and *Atherton* (DE-169) 30 miles south, picked up the signal even before the *Black Point* went down. LCDR L. B. Tollaksen, USCG, the senior officer present, ordered *Moberly* and the destroyer escorts to proceed to the scene, pending further instructions from Commander, Task Group 60.7, aboard destroyer *Ericsson* (DD-440) enroute to Boston via the Cape Cod Canal.

USS MOBERLY (PF-63).

Naval Historical Center photo.

The three warships reached the area of the sinking about 7:30 p.m. and promptly proceeded to form a scouting line. Their plan was to search in a southerly direction along the most likely route to be chosen by the submarine. *Atherton* made sonar contact seven miles south and by 8:30 p.m. commenced dropping depth charges. In the interim *Amick* left for another assignment. *Atherton* then made two runs with hedgehogs but lost contact with the submarine after the second attack. Destroyer *Ericsson* arrived shortly thereafter and established a barrier patrol with other naval ships to prevent the submarine from escaping.

USS ATHERTON (DE-169).

National Archives photo 80-G-325232.

The barrier force comprised the USS *Action*, the USS *Barney* (DD-149), the USS *Breckenridge* (DD-148), the USS *Blakely* (DD-150), the USS *Newport* (PF-27), the USS *Restless* (PG-66) and the USS *Semmes* (AG-24).

Sometime after 11:30 p.m., *Atherton* picked up a sonar signal about two miles east of its first point of contact with the submarine and initiated a third hedgehog attack. Soon afterward, air bubbles, oil and debris rose to the surface. *Atherton* maintained contact and made another run with depth charges. Using searchlights, *Atherton* and *Moberly* searched the area briefly for wreckage and debris, recovering various objects from the water including a life jacket and a pillow. The attack on the submerged U-boat resumed shortly afterward with *Atherton* making the first run. In following, *Moberly* reported the target moving across her bow at a speed of four to five knots. At about 2:00 a.m., after additional hedgehog runs, the movement of the submarine had slowed to a crawl. No further attacks were made for the rest of the night. Ships searching the area reported an oil slick extending a half mile from the area of the last attack and heavy concentrations of oil and air bubbles rising to the surface. All types of debris were retrieved from the water, including life jackets and rafts, escape lungs, survival kits, and also an officer's cap.

USS MOBERLY (PF-63) in antisubmarine action, May 6, 1945.

National Archives photo 26-G-4555.

Antisubmarine action off Rhode Island coast, May 6, 1945.
National Archives photo 26-G-4557.

Two blimps, the K-16 and K-58 from Lakehurst, New Jersey, arrived at dawn on May 6 and assisted in pinpointing the location of the submarine, which was then in a stationary position at 130 feet. Additional attacks were ordered until it could be ascertained through the use of sonobuoys that the submarine had indeed been destroyed. The action was completed by 10:45 a.m. Practice hedgehog runs continued for two more hours before the naval vessels left the scene.

Later in the day a diver from USS *Penguin* (ASR-12) identified the sunken submarine as the U-853. She was lying on the bottom, seven and one-half miles east of Block Island, her side and hull split open and crew entombed within. U-853, one of the last German submarines to reach the U.S. coastal area during World War II, had made her final and fatal attack on the *Black Point* off the Rhode Island shoreline just 28 hours before Germany surrendered to allied forces at Rheims, France, ending the war in Europe.

At Fort Greene the alert was cancelled and once again all was calm and quiet.

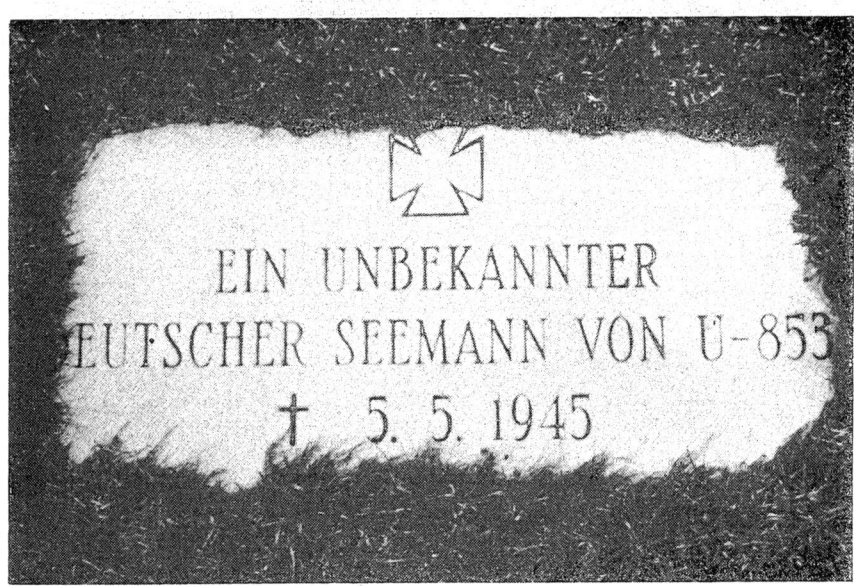

When private interests brought up the skeletal remains of a crew member of the U-853 in 1960, the U. S. Navy provided for proper burial services.

Photo of Naval Photographic Center.

Photo by author

Propellers of U-853 were brought ashore after the war.

Photo by author.

American, British, and German war dead found their final resting place in Newport, not far from where they perished.

Photo by author.

UNREALIZED POTENTIAL

Germany launched its first "buzz bombs" against England from sites on the European continent in June 1944. Known as the V-1, these expendable long-range pilotless bombers could have presented a serious threat to the U.S. coastal region if they had been adapted for launching from submarines. This potential never materialized, however. That such a weapon was within the realm of realization in World War II is evidenced by Japan's development of several classes of gigantic submarines, some in excess of 6,600 tons, capable of carrying from two to four bomber-type aircraft, each with a 1,600-pound bombload. Designed to bomb the Panama Canal and American cities, the destructive potential of these weapons systems was never put to the test either.

Japanese submarine of the I-400 Class with aircraft catapult on forward deck.

National Archives photo 80 G-389158.

A prototype of German JU-390 aircraft which was being tested in transport, reconnaissance, and bomber configurations.

Photo courtesy of Imperial War Museum, London, England.

Transport configuration of the JU-390 long-range reconnaissance aircraft.

U. S. Air Force photo.

Another possible menace to the U.S. coastal area which also never came to fruition was Germany's JU-390 long-range heavy bomber and reconnaissance aircraft. This six-engine plane had a capability of carrying a 4,255-pound bombload. A test flight originating at an airfield in France brought one of these planes within 12 miles of the coast north of New York in 1944. The aircraft returned safely to its base. The rapidly changing situation in the European Theater of Operations in favor of the Allies and the increasing tempo of bombing raids on Germany contributed substantially to the enemy's inability to further develop the potential of this long-range strategic aircraft.

The highly destructive V-2 rocket, first launched against England from the Netherlands in September 1944, was the forerunner of a long-range missile the Germans planned to fire at the United States. At that late date in the war, however, the enemy was no longer in a position to perfect this weapon for its intended purpose.

SELECTED POWs WITH A MISSION

During World War II close to 370,000 German prisoners of war were interned in 378 camps across the United States. Most of the POWs had been members of Field Marshal Rommel's Afrika Korps, the cream of Germany's manhood. The Army estimated that 15% of these men were Nazis, another 15% anti-Nazis, and the remaining 70% fellow travelers, afraid to speak out and be heard. Recognizing that these young men would eventually become one of the most influential groups in post-war Germany, the Army in 1943 explored the feasibility of exposing the majority of the prisoners to some form of political re-education. Although the idea had potential value, the Army was inexperienced with this type of psychological warfare. If the program were not carried out discreetly, the risk of retaliation against American prisoners in German captivity had to be considered, as well as a possible violation of the terms of the Geneva Convention. In view of these circumstances, program implementation was shelved.

In the meantime, captive Nazi officers were ruling some of the POW compounds in the United States with an iron fist, vehemently upholding the teachings and principles of the Third Reich supported by their local camp newspapers. In these camps readings from Hitler's *Mein Kampf* were placed high on the agenda of internal educational/enlightenment programs. Strong-arm tactics were employed against fellow prisoners who dared disagree with the philosophy of the regime. A series of crimes, including hangings, forced suicides, and numerous beatings were reported among the POWs. Generally the victims had been found guilty of treason by a Court of Honor convened in the safety of the POW compounds by the politically powerful Nazi elements. Although these conditions were not prevelent throughout all camps, the disturbing news of the operation of German kangaroo courts on U.S. soil and of the political intimidation among POWs reached the White House in March 1944. Eleanor Roosevelt took a personal interest in the reports and upon investigation became a staunch advocate of a political reorientation program for German prisoners of war. The President supported the idea. Soon after, the Army revived its earlier plans; however, the delicate nature of the project dictated that any political countermeasures aimed at Nazi elements within the camps be shrouded in secrecy.

During the summer of 1944, Major General Archer L. Lerch, then Provost Marshal General of the Army, implemented the POW re-education program, aided by Brigadier General Blackshear M. Bryan, Jr., Assistant Provost Marshal General. Lieutenant Colonel Edward Davison, a former professor at the University of Colorado and an internationally known educator, poet, and author, was given the job of getting the program off the ground. He was made director of the Special Projects Division, a newly formed group within the POW Division of the Provost Marshal General's Office created for this purpose.

The Geneva Convention which governed the treatment of prisoners of war allowed the captor nation to provide its prisoners with "intellectual diversion," provided the prisoners were receptive to such activity. To accomplish the goals of the re-education program, the influence the Nazis were exerting within the camps had to be neutralized early in the process. This was achieved by identifying the hard-core fanatics, separating them from the general POW population, and finally moving them to isolated camps.

Commencing in November 1944, specially selected and qualified American officers with knowledge of Germany's language and customs were called to Fort Slocum, N.Y., where in complete secrecy they were briefed on the re-education project. When the period of indoctrination was completed, each of these men was assigned to a POW camp as Assistant Executive Officer, responsible for the general re-education of the prisoners through the use of radio, newspapers, and entertainment. Concurrently, the Special Projects Division set up an "idea factory" at the abandoned Civilian Conservation Corps camp at Van Etten in upper New York State, where a staff of American scholars and intellectuals, both civilian and military, was joined by a small group of highly educated German POWs whose anti-Nazi leanings had been verified through an intensive screening process. The group collaborated in exploring methods of teaching the German prisoners the principles of democracy. This effort supported those of the Assistant Executive Officers who were being trained at Fort Slocum. Among the accomplishments of the Van Etten Group was the initial publication of the bi-weekly newspaper *Der Ruf (The Call)*, written for German POWs by fellow prisoners. The first issue, dated March 1, 1945, was distributed to all camp canteens, where it could be purchased by the prisoners on a voluntary basis at a nominal cost of five cents. So as not to reveal the location of the editorial staff, *Der Ruf* listed a post office box in New York City as return address. The paper was printed at a classified military installation in Washington, D. C. The Army had planned two more projects in addition to the general re-education program being undertaken at the individual camps, namely, those of preparing selected POWs for administrative positions as civil servants in postwar Germany and of training a cadre of civil police officers who would assist allied military authorities following cessation of hostilities.

Since the facilities at Van Etten were inadequate, the operations were transferred to Fort Kearney in Saunderstown, Rhode Island, in March 1945. The Narragansett Bay area was chosen since several harbor defense installations were then being evacuated by the Coast Artillery. It was therefore possible for the Special Projects Division to acquire critically needed space and facilities with the potential for expansion with the least amount of disruption.

Captain Robert L. Kunzig, USA, was the Commanding Officer of the Fort Kearney project, a clandestine operation that became known as "The Factory" in Army circles. Eighty-five specially selected POWs carried on Van Etten's editorial functions of *Der Ruf*. This centrally controlled POW newspaper ultimately reached a circulation of 75,000 copies. The Kearney staff also kept its fingers on the pulse of POW opinion by reviewing and translating into English approximately 80 local camp newspapers. In addition, the group reviewed magazines, books, films and plays for content and made recommendations on the advisability of making these materials available for general POW consumption. Among the literature suggested were the works of several prominent authors whose books had been banned and publicly burned in Nazi Germany.

The only person in Rhode Island having firsthand knowledge of the program during the early months of the POW presence was Governor J. Howard McGrath. He was kept apprised of developments by the Commander of Fort Kearney, who acted as the Army's emissary.

In May 1945, sixty prisoners volunteered to participate in a pilot program of the second project, i.e., a 60-day indoctrination in the principles of democratic government. Among the subjects studied were the English language, government, civics and geography. Dr. Howard Mumford Jones, President of the Academy of Arts and Sciences and a professor at Harvard University on loan to the Army, was instrumental in organizing and overseeing this effort. The group graduated on July 6.

With the successful conclusion of the test, the Narragansett Bay area became for a period of approximately one year the center of the most long-range and idealistic POW re-education efforts ever undertaken by the United States.

Ten of the Kearney graduates were promptly transferred to Cherbourg, France, where they functioned as instructors of fellow prisoners at a similar school in operation nearby.

In June, while the pilot program was still in progress at Fort Kearney, the Army officially established the School of Administration at Fort Getty on Conanicut Island. The first group of pre-selected German POWs was transferred to this site in time to commence classes in July.

Major John M. Moore, USA, was assigned as Camp Commander. He had at his disposal a service company of German prisoners, who were brought in to maintain the facilities and provide essential services to the school. Approximately 90 war prisoners were assigned to a barracks that had previously housed 65 GIs. A minimum amount of security was maintained, with only barbed wire fencing being erected around the bunkhouses.

Fort Getty in 1945. View from the East.

Photo courtesy Col. M. S. McKnight.

The Army School Center set up operations at Fort Getty under the command of Lt. Col. Alpheus W. Smith, a former professor of English. The school established two libraries and utilized several study rooms and the theater for its programs. The vacant Army Station Hospital built just outside the gate of the fort area in 1941 was converted into an educational complex of 56 classrooms and a language laboratory. The final curriculum of the administrative school included language, military government, German history and American history. Groups of 160-180 Germans passed through the school every 60 days.

Headquarters for the prisoner of war school at Fort Getty.
U. S. Navy photo courtesy Mrs. Lauretta N. Smith.

General Dwight D. Eisenhower, Supreme Commander of Allied Forces in Europe, had accepted suggestions made in 1944 to utilize handpicked Germans to assist military government officials and the Military Police in carrying out their duties in occupied Germany after the war. Ten teams from the Provost Marshal General's Office visited every German prisoner-of-war camp in the United States, testing and interviewing approximately 18,000 avowed anti-Nazis in search of several thousand likely candidates. Many of the potential selectees had been members of the 999th Division of the Afrika Korps, a punitive unit that surrendered in Tunisia in 1943. This unit had consisted of hard-core criminals, as well as men who had been branded as political opponents of the regime in Germany. Many had served in concentration camps, and, in the eyes of Hitler's men, all were enemies of the Nazi society. The search team had the task of seeking out the anti-Nazis while simultaneously screening and eliminating the criminals from further consideration. The task was not an easy one, and in some instances it became necessary to resort to the use of lie detectors. Roughly 3,000 prisoners were finally selected to attend the special POW schools.

The Station Hospital at Fort Getty, newly constructed in 1941, became a language laboratory for German prisoners of war in 1945.

National Archives photo, RG-77.

Forty percent of the students were officers. The highest rank held by these men was Lieutenant Colonel. All had waived their rights and privileges as officers as a prerequisite to participating in the program. They, along with the other POW students, were treated as civilians and addressed as such. The student body consisted primarily of well-educated professionals, including teachers, business executives, lawyers, engineers, editors, accountants, bankers, actors and clerks, as well as a smaller number of mechanics, farmers and tradesmen.

The third educational project instituted by the Provost Marshal General was the establishment under the Army School Center of a Police School at Fort Wetherill on August 27, 1945. Major Kenneth K. Kolster, USA, was the director of this new operaton. The POW student body in this instance was comprised primarily of former police officers, judges and others previously associated with or interested in police work. The group studied history and government, with special emphasis placed on law and its enforcement. The two-month course involved 30 days of academic study and 30 days of police training. Guest lecturers from federal, state and local police and law enforcement agencies participated actively in the educational process of the POWs. Well-qualified Germans also assisted as instructors.

Graduation of German prisoners of war at the U. S. Army School Center, Fort Getty, November 30, 1945.

Navy photo courtesy W. G. Moulton.

On September 18, 1945, one month after Japan's surrender, the Army invited the press to Fort Getty for briefings on the re-education projects and a tour of the facilities. Every major newspaper in the country subsequently related the story of this far-reaching program. Selected prisoners of war, later invited to make public appearances, hailed the Army's effort as a success.

Approximately 70 faculty members had been assigned to the Army School Center. They were mostly officers and enlisted personnel with outstanding records of academic accomplishments. Many had distinguished careers as professors and instructors at some of the nation's best universities and colleges. A few exceptionally qualified civilians were also included on the staff. With such academic excellence it is understandable that the POW School Center was referred to by the press as a "Barbed Wire College" and a "School of Democracy." Despite these excellent credentials, the program and the instruction personnel drew expressions of disapproval and distrust from some quarters who suspected the program of being too liberal.

Unfortunately, the accusations resulted in the disintegration of the program. Transfers, discharges and personnel reassignments followed. The police school was deactivated on November 30, 1945, and the last class of special students to graduate from Fort Getty began their homeward journey on December 16. The 130 members of the POW Service Company were subsequently processed through the school before being repatriated. A total of 1,166 German prisoners of war graduated from the Fort Getty/Wetherill school complex. Each participant received a Certificate of Achievement for "successfully completing the training course for Prisoners of War conducted at Fort Getty, Rhode Island, and established for the education of selected citizens of Germany."

Final issue of "DER RUF."

Photo courtesy Karl J. R. Arndt Archives, Clark University.

The World War II experience ended in the Narragansett Bay area when the last prisoners of war passed through the gate they had built at Fort Getty on their way back to Germany.

Photo by author.

While the Fort Getty operation was phasing out, another re-education project was being organized at Fort Eustis, Virgina. Several former members of the Getty staff were again hard at work, this time processing more than 20,000 prisoners through a series of abbreviated crash courses in less than four months. The editorial staff of *Der Ruf* continued operations in Rhode Island until publication of the 26th and final issue on April 1, 1946, which coincided with the conclusion of the re-education program at Fort Eustis.

With the departure of the last German prisoners of war from Fort Kearney, the World War II experience of the Narragansett Bay area came to an end.

APPENDIX

The following are excerpts from the General Orders and other directives referred to on pages 68 to 71.

Assignments of the 10th and 243rd Coast Artillery Regiments in accordance with General Order No. 26 and Change 1, dated December 13 and 31, 1943:

Organization		Armament	Location
10th Coast Artillery			
Battery 'A'	Mine Command No. 2		East Passage
Battery 'B'	Mine Command No. 1		West Passage
Battery 'C'	AMTB No. 3	4-90mm 2-37mm	Brenton Point
Battery 'D'	Battery Gray	2-16" BC	Fort Church
Battery 'E'	Battery Reilly	2-8" BC	Fort Church
Battery 'F'	Battery No. 212	2-6" BC	Fort Church
Battery 'G'	Searchlights		Aquidneck Island and East Bay area
243rd Coast Artillery			
Battery 'A'	Battery House	2-6" BC	Fort Varnum
Battery 'B'	Battery No. 213	2-6" BC	Fort Burnside
Battery 'C'	AMTB No. 1	2-90mm Fixed 2-37mm	Fort Varnum Fort Kearney
Battery 'E'	Battery Hamilton	2-16" BC	Fort Greene
Battery 'F'	Battery No. 211	2-6" BC	Fort Greene
Battery 'G'	AMTB No. 4	2-90mm Mobile	Fort Wetherill
Battery 'H'	AMTB No. 5	2-90mm Mobile	Fort Adams
Battery 'I'	AMTB No. 2	2-90mm Fixed	Fort Getty
Battery 'K'	Searchlights		Conanicut Island and West Bay area

It should be noted that Battery 'D' of the 243rd had been reassigned to duty in Maine in June 1943.

Reorganization of the 243rd Coast Artillery Regiment in accordance with General Order No. 7 of February 22, 1944:

FROM	TO	ASSIGNMENT	STATION	STATUS
Hqs/Hqs Battery	No Change	Harbor Defense Command Post	Fort Getty	
Hqs Bty 1st Bn	No Change	Group 3 AA-AMTB	Brenton Point	
Battery 'A'	Battery 'F'	AMTB-3	Brenton Point	
'B'	'E'	AMTB-1	Fort Varnum	
'C'	'H'	Battery 212	Fort Church	
Hqs Bty 2nd Bn	No Change	Group 1	Fort Greene	
'E'	'B'	Battery 213	Fort Burnside	
'F'	'C'	Battery 211	Fort Greene	
Hqs Bty 3rd Bn	No Change	Group 2 (6" Group)	Fort Varnum	Surplus
'G'	'A'	MC-1 and MC-2	Fort Wetherill	
'H'	'K'	Battery House	Fort Varnum	
'I'	No Change	AMTB-2	Fort Getty	Surplus
'K'	'G'	All Searchlights	Fort Adams	Surplus
Medical	No Change		Fort Getty	
Band	No Change		Fort Getty	Surplus

With Headquarters Battery 3rd Battalion being declared surplus, the Regiment from this point forward operated with only two battalions.

The reorganization of the 243rd Coast Artillery Regiment under General Order No. 29 of September 29, 1944 and formation of the 188th and 189th Coast Artillery Battalions (HD).:

FROM	TO	ASSIGNMENT	LOCATION
243rd CA (HD) Hqs Battery, 1st Bn	188th CA (HD) Hqs & Hqs Detachment		Fort Wetherill
Battery 'A'	Battery 'A'	Mine	East/West Passage
'B'	'B'	6" Gun No. 213	Fort Burnside
'C'	'C'	6" Gun No. 211	Fort Greene
'H'	'D'	6" Gun No. 212	Fort Church
Hqs & Hqs Battery	189th CA Bn (HD) Hqs & Hqs Detachment		Fort Adams
Battery 'E'	Battery 'A'	AMTB	Forts Varnum/Kearney
'F'	'B'	AMTB (Alert)	Fort Wetherill
'G'	'C'	Searchlights	Various

Reorganization of the Harbor Defenses of Narragansett Bay in accordance with Headquarters Northeastern Sector General Order No. 5 of March 29, 1945:

OLD DESIGNATION	NEW DESIGNATION
Hqs & Hqs Battery Harbor Defenses of Narragansett Bay	Same
Battery 'A' - 188th CA Bn	Battery 'A' Harbor Defenses of Narragansett Bay
Battery 'C' - 189th CA Bn	Battery 'B' HD of Narragansett Bay
Battery 'C' - 188th CA Bn	Battery 'C' HD of Narragansett Bay
Battery 'D' - 188th CA Bn	Battery 'D' HD of Narragansett Bay

BIBLIOGRAPHY

An Administrative History of PT's in WW II. Washington, D.C.: Office of Naval History, 1946.

Andersch, Alfred. "Getty." In *Interview mit Amerika.* Ed. Alfred Gong. Nymphenburger Verlagshandlung, Germany, 1962, pp. 351-61.

Arndt, Karl J. R., and May E. Olsen. *The German Language Press of the Americas. 1732-1968.* Vol. ll. Munich, Germany: Verlag Dokumentation, 1973.

Arnold, S. G. *History of the State of Rhode Island.* 3rd ed. Vol II. New York: D. Appleton & Company, 1878.

Baldwin, Hanson W. "Submarines Studied." *New York Times,* April 3, 1946, p. 11.

The Bay Islands Park: A Marine Recreation Plan for the State of Rhode Island. University of Rhode Island, Coastal Resources Center, n.d.

Bibliothek Für Zeitgeschichte, Stuttgart, Germany. Letter to author. October 24, 1978.

Bogart, Charles H. "New England Frontier Defense Sector: 1941-1945." *WW2 Journal,* Bennington, Vermont. Vol 3, No. 1 (January-February 1976).

The Book of Newport, Rhode Island. Fort Adams, Rhode Island: U. S. Government Institutions, Newport Service Society, 1930.

Building the Navy's Bases in World War II: History of the Bureau of Yards and Docks and the Civil Engineer Corps, 1940-1946. Vol. I. Washington, D.C.: Bureau of Yards and Docks, GPO, 1947.

Bulkley, Robert J., Jr., Captain USNR (Ret.). *At Close Quarters — PT Boats in the United States Navy.* Washington, D.C.: Naval History Division, GPO, 1962.

"Captives Trained to Police Germany." *New York Times,* September 23, 1945, p. 23.

Cloney, Will. "Salvaging Germans for Democracy." *Liberty Magazine,* December 8, 1945, pp. 26-27, 84-85.

"Coast Defenses Marked as Good." *Providence Journal,* June 19, 1941, p. 5.

"Commandant First Naval District." *History of Naval Administration, World War II.* Vols. I-XI. Boston, 1946.

Conn, Stetson, Rose C. Engleman, and Byron Fairchild. *Guarding the United States and Its Outposts.* Washington, D.C.: GPO, 1964.

Construction Completion Reports. Washington, D.C.: National Archives, RG 77.

"Criminologist Says Lie Tests Used on Fort Getty POWs." *Providence Evening Bulletin,* August 25, 1945, p. 9.

Cruising Guide to Historic Rhode Island. University of Rhode Island, April 1976.

"Dedication Held for Fort Varnum." *Providence Journal,* April 19, 1943, p. 15.

Department of the Army. Center of Military History. HRC 331 Posts. Vols. 13, 14, 19, 36.

"Farewell to Famous Forts." *Providence Journal,* June 28, 1931.

Field, Edward. *Revolutionary Defenses in Rhode Island.* Providence, Rhode Island: Preston & Rounds, 1896.

"Fort Church Accepted." *Providence Journal,* April 30, 1940, p. 24.

"Fort Nathaneal Greene." *Providence Journal,* September 12, 1940, p. 14.

"14 Dead in Two U-Boat Sinkings Off East Coast as V-E Neared." *New York Times,* May 10, 1945, p. 1.

Frederiksen, Robert C. "The Killing of the U-853." *Providence Journal,* February 22, 1961.

Furer, Julius A. *Administration of the Navy Department in World War II.* Washington: GPO, 1959.

Gansberg, Judith M. *STALAG: U.S.A.* New York: Thomas Y. Crowell, 1977.

"German POWs in U.S. Compare Our Democracy with Fascism." *The Washington Daily News,* June 15, 1945, p. 28.

"German Prisoners Get Training at 3 Narragansett Bay Forts." *Providence Journal,* August 7, 1945, p. 22.

"German P.W.s to be Carriers of Democracy." *New York Herald Tribune,* September 29, 1945.

Gleeson, Paul F. *Rhode Island: The Development of Democracy.* Providence, Rhode Island: Rhode Island State Board of Education, Oxford Press, 1957.

Green, William. *Bombers.* Vol. X of *War Planes of the Second World War.* Garden City, New York: Doubleday & Company.

Greenberg, Selig. "Anti-Nazi POW's, Students of Liberty Say 'Americans Even Criticize Themselves' " *Providence Evening Bulletin,* September 22, 1945, p. 7.

Harbor Defense Project, Narragansett Bay, February 1, 1945. HDNARB-AN-45. Washington, D.C.: Records of the Adjutant General's Office, National Archives, RG407.

Harbor Defense Project, Narragansett Bay. AG No. 417. CCA-AN-N ARB-38. Annex "A". Washington, D.C.: Records of the Adjutant General's Office, National Archives, RG 407.

Herrick, Genevieve Forbes. "Behind Barbed Wire." *The Rotarian,* 1946.

Historical and Pictorial Review, National Guard of the State of R.I. Baton Rouge: Army Navy Publishing Company, 1940.

Historical Data Cards, 10th Coast Artillery Regiment. Washington. D.C.: National Archives, RG 407.

"History of Fort Adams." Unpublished Manuscript. Newport, Rhode Island: Naval War College Archives.

"How the Big Guns Work." *Providence Evening Bulletin,* February 3, 1941.

Hull, George C. "Now It Can Be Told." *Providence Evening Bulletin,* May 17, 1945.

Johnson, Stanley J. F. "179 German POWs Graduated at Ceremonies at Fort Getty." *Providence Sunday Journal,* October 21, 1945, p. 1.

King, Ernest J., Fleet Admiral. *U.S. Navy at War: 1941-1945.* Washington, D.C.: U.S. Navy Department, 1946.

King, Ernest J., and Walter M Whitehill. *Fleet Admiral King, a Naval Record.* New York: Norton, 1952.

Kirchner, D. P., Commander, USN and Captain E. R. Lewis, USAR. *American Harbor Defenses: The Final Era.* United States Naval Institute Proceedings, January 1968.

Lewis, Emanuel R. *Seacoast Fortifications of the United States.* Washington, D.C.: Smithsonian Institute Press, 1970.

Martasian, Paul. "Germans Depart for Fatherland." *Providence Sunday Journal,* December 16, 1945, p. 17.

McPartland, Martha R. *The History of East Greenwich, Rhode Island: 1677-1960.* East Greenwich: East Greenwich Free Library Association, 1960.

Military Reservations, National Cemeteries and Military Parks. Washington, D.C.: Army Office of the Judge Advocate General, GPO, 1916.

Military Reservations — Rhode Island, 1937-1942. Series of Pamphlets by State. Washington, D.C.: War Department, GPO, June 2, 1941.

Moore, John Hammond. "Hitler's Afrika Korps ... in New England." Dublin, New Hampshire: *Yankee Magazine,* June 1976, pp. 82-89, 116.

Morison, Samuel Eliot. "The Battle of the Atlantic: 1939-1943." In *History of United States Naval Operations in World War II.* Vol. I. Boston: Little, Brown and Company, 1956.

————. "The Atlantic Battle Won: May 1943-May 1945." In *History of United States Naval Operations in World War II.* Vol. X. Boston: Little, Brown and Company, 1956.

Munro, Wilfred H. "Picturesque Rhode Island." Providence, Rhode Island: J.A. and R.A. Reid, 1881, p. 294.

NAS Quonset Point, R.I. Commemorative Edition: July 12, 1944 — June 28, 1974. East Greenwich, Rhode Island: William A. Foster, Pendulum, June, 26, 1974.

"National Guard Starts Training at Fort Adams." *Newport Daily News,* September 23, 1940.

Naval Torpedo Station, Newport, Rhode Island. Vol. I. Washington, D.C.: Bureau of Ordnance, 1946.

The Navy in Newport. Unofficial Directory and Guide. San Diego, California: Military Publishers, 1977.

"Navy Tells How U-Boat Was Sunk Off Block Island." *Providence Evening Bulletin,* May 17, 1945.

"Nazis Sink Collier Near Point Judith." *Newport Daily News,* May 9, 1945, p. 1.

Newport Navalog. Special Navy Day Edition. Newport, Rhode Island: Edward A. Sherman Publishing Co., October 8, 1975.

"100,000 Cheer National Guard As 243rd Leaves for Newport." *Providence Journal,* September 23, 1940, p. 1.

Parkman, Aubrey. *Army Engineers in New England, 1775-1975.* Waltham, Massachusetts: U.S. Army Corps of Engineers, 1978.

The Passing Years, 1791-1966. Providence, Rhode Island: Industrial National Bank, 1966.

"Picked German Prisoners Win 'OK Degree' in School of Democracy." *The Christian Science Monitor,* September 21, 1945, p. 11.

Post, Camps & Station Files. Washington, D.C.: Fort Record Books, National Archives, RG 338.

"P.O.W.'s Taught to Govern Reich." *New York Sun,* September 21, 1945, p. 8.

Pratt, Fletcher. *The Compact History of the United States Navy.* 3rd ed. Hawthorne Books, 1967.

"Prisoner of War Camp Officials Address Rotary Club in Newport." *Providence Journal*, August 22, 1945.

"Regimental Drill Postponed." *Newport Daily News*, September 25, 1940.

Rhode Island. American Guide Series. Boston: Houghton Mifflin, 1937.

Roach, Thomas, and Elliott Subervi. "The Twisted Fate of the U-853." *Skin Diver Magazine*, March 1974.

Robinson, Willard B. "Adams — American Example of French Military Architecture." *Rhode Island Historical Society*, Vol. 34:3, August 1975.

————. *Report of the Restoration of Fort Adams*. Rhode Island State Department of Natural Resources, June 1972.

Rohwer, Jürgen. *Die U-Boot Erfolge Der Achsenmächte, 1939-1945*.

"School for POWs Will Be Closed." *The Providence Sunday Journal*, December 16, 1945.

Skordiles, Kimon. *The Seabees in Peace and War*. California: Argus Communications, Inc., 1973.

Steinberg, Sheila, and Cathleen McGuigan. *Rhode Island: An Historical Guide*. Providence, 1976.

Swanberg, W.A. "The Spies Who Came in from the Sea." *American Heritage Magazine*, April 1970.

Tollaksen, D. M., Ens. USN. *Last Chapter for U-853*. Annapolis, Maryland: U. S. Naval Institute Proceedings. December 1960.

" 'Top Secret' Taboo Lifted: How P.O.W. Projects Grew." *The Christian Science Monitor*, September 21, 1945.

"Two More 'Cities' Mushroom in R. I.," *Providence Sunday Journal*, December 15, 1940, p. 9.

"U-Boat Sinking Off R. I. Related." Newport, Rhode Island, *The News*, May 17, 1945.

Ulanoff, Stanley M. *Illustrated Guide to U. S. Missiles and Rockets*. Garden City, New York: Doubleday & Company, 1962.

"United States Military Insignia." *National Geographic*, Vol. LXXXIII, No. 6 (June 1943).

United States Submarine Losses, World War II. Washington, D.C.: Naval History Division, 1963.

U.S. Naval History Division. *Dictionary of American Naval Fighting Ships*. Washington: GPO, 1976.

"War Dept. Tells Facts of Prison Schools." *Newport Daily News,* September 21, 1945, p. 1.

War Diary. U. S. Naval Supply Depot, Newport, Rhode Island, of April 1, 1944 for March 1944. File A12-1 (7) NT4-41/(50).

War Diary. USS Penguin (ASR-12) of June 11, 1945.

Ward, John. "160 in PW Class Get Certificates." *The Providence Sunday Journal,* December 2, 1945.

Warren, Pauline. PWs Trained in R. I. to Help Police Reich." *Boston American,* September 21, 1945, p. 4.

Wetherill, Webster K. *The Naming of Our Forts.* A paper read before the Jamestown, Rhode Island Historical Society, August 23, 1943.

Wheeler Robert L. "In the Harbor Forts, English at High Speed." *The Providence Sunday Journal,* September 23, 1945, Section VI.

Wilbour, Benjamin Franklin. "Notes on Little Compton." Little Compton Historical Society, 1970. In *Village Bell,* 1969, The United Congregational Church of Little Compton, Rhode Island.

Willoughby, Malcolm F. *U. S. Coast Guard in WW II.* Annapolis, Maryland: U. S. Naval Institute, 1957.

World War II Operational Reports, 243rd Coast Artillery Regiment. Washington, D.C.: National Archives, RG 407.

Wright, Sydney L. and Catharine M. *The Good Old Summer Time.* Compiled 1963; reprinted 1974.

Zander, Wolf Dieter. "Freedom and Barbed Wire." *Herald Tribune* "Forum," October 30, 1945.

INDEX

Act of Panama, 1
Advance Base Depot, 88, 90
Advance Base Proving Ground, 91
Administration School (POW), 114
Afrika Korps, 111
    999th Division, 115
Amagansett, Long Island, 100
Ammunition storage, 80
Antiaircraft, 13, 18, 41, 43, 45, 68, 70, 93-95
    Training Center, 75, 85
Anti-Motor Torpedo Boat Battery, 23, 32, 61, 68, 70
Army
    Mine planter, 18
    Schools Center (POW), 115, 117
    Station Hospital, 115
    Units *(numerical)*
        10th Coast Artillery, 3, 8, 9, 11, 18, 32, 33, 41, 61, 68
        13th Infantry, 11
        22nd Quartermaster, 32-33
        132nd Engineers, 32-33
        188th Coast Arty. Battalion, 18, 48, 70
        189th Coast Arty. Battalion, 70
        207th Coast Artillery (AA), 94-96
        243rd Coast Artillery (HD), 5-9, 11, 15, 18, 23, 32, 36, 41, 48, 50-51, 57, 61, 68-70
        540th Anti Aircraft Arty, 96
        701st Coast Artillery (AA), 95-96
Bailey, Lt. Leonard W., 82
Bar Harbor, 100
Base End Stations, 7, 50, 53
Battery Command Post, 51, 56, 61
Blimps, 80, 101, 106
Block Island, 3, 14, 43, 65, 102
Bonnet, The, 65
Boom, 58
Brenton Point, 3, 43, 56, 65, 70, 75
Bridge, 1st Lt. Harold E., 54
Bryan, Brig. Gen. Blackshear M., 112
Buzz bombs, 109
Camps
    Endicott, 90
    Thomas, 90
    Van Etten, 112, 113
Campbell, Brig. Gen. Arthur G., 67
Camouflage, 11
Cape Cod, 102-103
CEC Officers Training School, 91
Charlestown, 88
C.M.T.C. Site, Fort Adams, 7
Coast Artillery Units *(See Army)*
Coasters Harbor Island, 73, 94
Coast Guard, 56
    Hibiscus, 103
    Hornbeam, 103
    PE-63 *Moberley*, 103, 105
Coddington Cove, 72, 74, 79
Coddington Point, 73-74
Commons, Capt. William G., Jr., 64

Conanicut Island (Jamestown), 3, 8, 14, 21, 27, 31, 35-36, 39, 78, 114
Beaverhead, 21
Beavertail, 35, 53, 56-57, 70
Fox Hill, 21
Revolutionary battery, 35
Curry, CDR Ralph R., 100
Cuttyhunk, 43-45, 65
Daneker, Lt. Col. John L., 9
Datson, Lt. Col. John F., 6, 23
Davison, Lt. Col. Edward, 112
Davisville, 88, 91
Degaussing Station, 80
DeRita, Lt. Col. Joseph, 41, 64, 70
Doenitz, Grand Admiral, K., 102
Dolan, Major John R., 18
Dumplings, The, 14-15
Dutch Island, 3, 27, 28, 31
Earthworks, 35
Editorial staff (POW), 113
Eisenhower, General Dwight D., 115
Endicott
    Board, 9
    Camp, 90
    Secretary of War, 9
Factory, The, 113
Fall, CDR Andrew C., 87
Fall River, 3, 79
Fire Control Points, 35, 43-45, 53, 55, 61, 64
Forstot, Captain George, 48
Fortin, Major Thomas L., 48
Forts
    Adams, 3, 6-9, 15, 23, 35-36, 56, 67-70, 93
    Anne, 77
    Burnside, 23, 35, 39, 53, 56
    Church, 40, 43, 48, 61, 68, 71
    Eustis, 119
    Getty, 3, 8, 21, 23, 31-32, 36, 44, 56-58, 61, 68, 114-115, 117-118
    George, 77
    Greble, 3, 21, 27-28, 31
    Greene, 43-44, 46, 48, 50, 61, 68, 70-71, 102, 106
    Kearney, 3, 21, 23, 31, 36, 58, 68, 113-114, 119
    Liberty, 77
    Slocum, 112
    Varnum, 23, 32, 43-45, 61, 70
    Wolcott, 77
    Washington, 77
    Wetherill, 3, 8-9, 14-15, 18, 32, 35-36, 44, 48, 51, 58, 61, 68, 70, 93, 116
Fox Hill, 21
Frenchtown Military Reservatioin, 91
Frömsdorf, Oblt. Helmut, 101
Fuel Depot, 82
Gate tenders, 58, 83
Gay Head, 43, 65
Geneva Convention, 111-112
George, Col. Russel T., 23

German POWs, 111-119
Gilbert, Lt. Col. Oliver H., 41
Gilbert, 1st Lt. Sidney P., 41
Goat Island, 77-80, 93-95
Gooseberry Neck, 43-45, 65
Gould Island, 78-80, 87-88, 94-95
Green Hill, 43, 53, 65
Green, Senator Theodore Francis, 79
Gulbrandsen, Capt. Oskar S., 64
Gun batteries
  Named:
    Armistead, 23, 32
    Cooke, 18
    Cram, 32
    Crittenden, 15
    Dickenson, 15, 44, 61
    French, 31
    Gray, 42-44, 48
    Hale, 28
    Hamilton, 48, 50, 68
    House, 23, 44, 61
    Mitchell, 28
    Ogden, 28
    Reilly, 43-44
    Segewick, 28
    Toussard, 23
    Varnum, 15
    Walbach, 18
    Wheaton, 15
    Whiting, 23, 56
    Zook, 18
  Numbered:
    108, 48
    109, 50
    211, 51, 53, 61, 70, 102
    212, 44-45, 61, 68, 70
    213, 54, 61, 70
    921, 61
Gunnery range, 75, 85
Haines, Brig. Gen. Ralph E., 67
Harbor Defense
  Board, 37, 39-40
  Command, 56, 65, 67-68, 70
Harbor Entrance Control Post, 56-59
Hinternhoff, Major William A., 41
Hitler, Adolf, 111
Hope Island, 86
Hospital
  Army, 115
  Navy, 73
Ingersoll, Admiral Royal, 94
Jamestown (Conanicut Island), 3, 8, 14, 21, 27, 31, 35-36, 39
Jones, Howard Mumford, 114
Jones, Brig. Gen. Thomas H., 67
JU-390 aircraft, 110
Kalbfus, Rear Admiral Edward C., 87
King, Fleet Admiral Ernest J., 72
Kolster, Major Kenneth K., 116
Knox, Secretary of Navy Frank, 79
Kunzig, Captain Robert L., 113
Lerch, Major Gen Archer L., 112

Lighthouses
  Beavertail, 35, 53, 56
  Dutch Island, 27
  Point Judith, 51
Little Compton, 5, 37, 40, 48
Long Island, 3, 102
Luce, Commodore Stephen B., 73
McCachern, Major William Y., 18
McGrath, Governor J. Howard, 113
McGrath, Major Thomas W., 64
Martha's Vineyard, 43
Matthews, Commander E. O., 77
Mein Kampf, 111
Melville, 79, 82-84
Mine planter, Army, 18, 35
Moore, Lt. Col. Ernest W., 8, 23
Moore, Major John M., 114
MTB Squadrons Training Center, 79, 84
Narragansett Bay, 3, 5-6, 9, 15, 27-28, 37, 39, 53-54, 57, 65, 67-68, 72, 82, 85-86, 101, 113, 114
  East Passage, 3, 8, 11, 14, 56, 58, 77-78, 82, 83
  West Passage, 3, 21, 27, 57-58
Natali, Major Dean J., 41, 64
Naval Air Station, 72, 86-88, 93, 95
Naval Construction Battalions, 90
Naval Construction Training Center, 88, 90-91
Naval Fuel Depot, 82
Naval Magazine, 78, 80
Naval Net Depot, 82
Naval Operating Base, 82, 94
Naval Supply Depot, 72
Naval Torpedo Station, 77, 79, 81, 85
Naval Training Station, 72-73, 75, 83, 85, 87-88, 94, 95
Naval War College, 73
Navy loops, 57-58
Nazis, 111
Net Depot, 82
Neutrality Patrol, 87
Newport, 3, 7, 11, 14-15, 36, 67, 72-75, 77, 79, 82-83, 87, 93-94
  Eustis Avenue, 95
  Long Wharf, 79
  Ruggles Avenue, 95
North Kingstown, 86
Panama Detachment, 8-9
Panama mount, 53
Pearl Harbor, 40, 82
Peirce, Colonel C. P., 67
Pendleton, Lt. Col. Randolph T., 67
Point Judith, 3, 5, 14, 37, 43, 45-46, 48, 102-103
Police School (POW), 116
Ponte Vedra, Florida, 100
Pontoons, 91-92
Portsmouth, 82
Price's Neck, 75, 85
Prisoners of war, 111
  Re-education project, 111-119

Prospect Hill, 35
Providence, 3, 6, 72
Provost Marshal General, 112
Prudence Island, 3, 80
PT boats, 79, 84-85
QM Wharf, 18
Quidnessett, 86, 88
Quonset hut, 84, 92-93
Quonset Point, 72, 86-90, 93
Radar, 43-45, 50, 53, 55-57, 61, 64, 70
Re-education project (POW), 111
Reiber, Major Frederick E., 18
Rembijas, Captain John C., 48, 54
Reserve Officers Indoctrination, 74, 87
Rifle ranges, 28, 73, 75
Rhodes, Lt. Col. Frank B., 9, 18
Roever, Captain Frederick O., 48
Rommel, Field Marshal Erwin, 111
Roosevelt, Eleanor, 111
Roosevelt, President Franklin D., 1-2, 6, 79, 86, 112
Rose Island, 78, 95
Ruf, Der, 113, 119
Rumazza, Major Robert S., 18, 54
Sachuest Point, 43-45, 65, 70
Sakonnet Point, 5, 37, 39-40, 44, 46, 58
Saunderstown, 28, 31, 36, 113
Schimmel, Captain Bernard H., 41
Schmidt, Captain L., Jr., 33
Seabees, 88, 90
Searchlights, 8, 23, 57, 61, 64, 70, 95
Ship-Precommissioning, 74
Smith, Lt. Col. Alpheus W., 115
Snorkel, 97
Snyder, Captain George R., 33
Sommer, Kapitänleutnant Helmut, 101
South Ferry, 31
South Weymouth, 80
Specht, LCDR William C., 84.
Special Projects Division, 112
Spotters, 7
Spry, Lt. Col. Francis N., 18, 48, 70
Stagge, Captain William G., 64
State of emergency, 1, 79
Stern, Lt. Col. Isadore H., 41, 54
Stetson, 1st Lt. William E., 48
Submarines
    U-202, 100
    U-230, 100
    U-548, 101
    U-550, 99
    U-584, 100
    U-853, 101-102, 106
    U-857, 100
    U-1230, 100
Submarine net, 58, 82-83
Sun Valley, 91
Supply Station, 72
Sweeten, Captain Gomer A., 33
Taunton, 3
Tefft, Captain Donald R., 64
Thompson, Captain Frederick A. 41
Tobin, Colonel Ralph C., 94

Tollaksen, LCDR L. B., 103
Torpedo net, 82
Torpedo Station, 80, 93
Vanderbilt, Governor William H., 6
Vessels
  Commercial
    Aeolus, 98
    Alexander Macomb, 99
    Atlantic States, 100-101
    Belgian Airman, 101
    Ben & Josephine, 98
    Black Point, 99, 102-103, 106
    Cherokee, 98
    Cornwallis, 99
    Ebb, 99
    Kamen, 103
    Mattawin, 98
    Norness, 98
    Pan Pennsylvania, 99
    Port Nicholson, 99
    Skottland, 98
  Military
    USS AMP *General Absolom Baird*, 18
    USS *Action*, 104
    USS *Amick*, 103-104
    USS *Atherton*, 103-104
    USS *Barney*, 104
    USS *Blakely*, 104
    USS *Breckenridge*, 104
    USS *Constellation*, 73,94
    USS *Croatan*, 101
    USS *Ericsson*, 103, 104
    USS *Gandy*, 99
    USS *Gustafson*, 100
    USS *Moberley*, 103, 105
    USS *New Hampshire*, 73
    USS *Newport*, 104
    PE-56 *Eagle Boat*, 101-102
    USS *Penguin*, 106
    USS *Restless*, 104
    USS *Semmes*, 104
V-1 and 2 Weapons, 109, 111
Ward, Captain James A., 54, 64
Warren Point, 43-45, 65
Washington Naval Treaty, 37
Water supply, 28
Webster, Colonel Earl C., 6, 23, 67
Westerly, 6, 88
Wickham, Captain Kenneth G., 33
Woodruff, Major Gen. James A., 8